Vagabond

A horseback adventure from Bulgaria to Berlin

Jeremy James

This edition published by Merlin Unwin Books 2015
First published in 1991 by Pelham Books

Merlin Unwin Books
Palmers House
7 Corve Street
Ludlow
Shropshire
SY8 1DB

A CIP record of this book is available from the British Library.

Printed in the UK by Jellyfish Print Solutions Ltd

ISBN 978 1 910723 01 2

The photographs were taken by Cecilia Humphrys, unless otherwise specified.

Contents

Foreword

Jeremy James's easy-going style – as informal as chat leaning on the bar of a wayside drinking hall with a weather-eye for his grazing horse – is so much more often hit than miss that one can't help suspecting, after a time, that the philistinism or the pretence of it, that he scatters about his pages is a tease. He lets give-away sparks of cultivation escape. The oversights may make an aesthete moan, but the insights are instinctively sound and perceptive, always warm and generous and, again and again, extremely funny. He is particularly adept at piecing together the companionable blinds and hangovers of one's youthful travels in wild places but the heroes of the book are neither the author, nor the denizens of south-eastern Europe, nor the landscape but the two steeds he bought off the gypsies in Bulgaria and Rumania.

These pages are hard to beat and, here and there, the reader's eyes prickle as though we were reading *Black Beauty* for the first time, in the gorges of the Great Balkan Range, or in the Carpathian uplands or on the Puszta.

We are carried in his wake across the Puszta, through Slovakia and the plains of Poland and through Eastern and Western Germany at a time of great political change. There are moments of doubt and acute anxiety, but by the time he is safe home in the Welsh mountains all early reservations have vanished and the author has us eating out of his hand.

Patrick Leigh Fermor

Now a horse is a fine lady among animals, flighty, timid, delicate in eating, of tender health: he is too valuable, too sensitive to be left alone, so that you are chained to your brute as to a fellow galley-slave: a dangerous road puts him out of his wits; in short, he's an uncertain and exacting ally and adds thirty-fold to the troubles of the voyager...

Travels with a Donkey in the Cevennes
Robert Louis Stevenson

Off

'I'm sorry to telephone you on a Saturday afternoon but my friend has done good work in Sofia and has found you two horses, one black, one white.' It was Mr Popof from the Bulgarian Embassy.

I'd asked for black and white horses: that is to say, piebald.

'Ah.'

'The white one is eight years old, the black one is also eight years old.'

'Ah.' 'You can BUY them in Sofia and the price is – how can I say? – the price is – er I cannot think – the price is, must be, let me see, with all saddles and bridles and everything – all you need is riding boots and breeches!'

'Ah.'

'The price is very good, what is? Hello? – maybe, well, maybe ... about ... 5 or maybe 8,000 dollars ... Hello? Hello? Mr Dchames? Hello? Of course these figures can be discussed and you can ... in Sofia ... Hello? Mr Dchames? Hello?'

'Strewth.'

'See you in Heathrow Mr Dchames?'

'Strewth.' And outside the sun was roaring away, bulbs in the garden were exploding, a thrush was singing and lambs were bawling their heads off. I didn't have 5 or 8,000 dollars. Not any more. I did, once, for a while: a short while, just after Pelham gave it to me. But what with one thing and another it'd gone. Advances are like that. Now you have them, now you don't. Now I didn't. What could I do?

This was serious worrying time: a bit of a jam. Thing was, I didn't want to go anyway, not with all that sunshine and spring.

Then a thought occurred: I thought maybe, maybe the money, or lack of it, was the way out. Maybe I'd just have to go to Bulgaria, then ring Roger in Pelham to tell him I couldn't do this ride because it was too expensive and he'd say 'OK, forget it' so I could come back and loaf around here all summer instead.

But it wasn't that easy.

Thing was I'd gone and committed myself in other ways: like Gonzo, my horse, for instance. I'd found him another home. And Dolly my Welsh pony and Punch my bull terrier, they'd got homes.

I set out to ride Gonzo to Norfolk to the ILPH (International League for the Protection of Horses) but sixteen miles down the road wound up in Jane Lennox's place and Jane wound up with Gonzo. Sixteen miles.

Dolly went home to Alan Watkin, her rightful owner – just across the fields from here – and Punch was in Devon with Mark Alderson, and Mark was going through this divorce business, hadn't got himself a house sorted out and already had a bull terrier anyway. And what worried me about it was Mark knew Punch, and knew about his funny little habits, so why did he agree to it? I mean why did he want to look after him? I know about Punch's funny little habits too. I have to pay for them. I had to pay for a new seat for Sid's motorbike, and for his tractor door, and for Sue's sofa to be restuffed and for her feather cushions to be restuffed and her elderly teddy bear to be restuffed. I just knew if I went away I'd come home to a massive restuffing bill. But it was done now, and he was in Devon, Gonzo was with Jane and Dolly was across the fields.

So, with all my animals gone, and air tickets bought, I was badly committed and everybody was expecting me to go.

Jeff Aldridge was expecting me to go. He said so one night when I was at his place round about closing time, down at The Crown. He got quite interested in me going. He said so. In fact he got very excited about it.

'Go away!' he said, 'Go on! Get out! Go away! And don't come back for six months!'

He even helped me to the door.

Who can resist encouragement like that?

So there I was mooching around in the garden one Saturday afternoon in all this sunshine and missing my animals when Mr Popof rang, which seemed to put the lid on everything, so I locked up the cottage, slung the saddles and saddlebags in the car, and went down to the Cotswolds to Chumpie, who was coming along. So she thought.

I drove a glorious sunny two hours to Gloucestershire and arrived to find her faffing about in a pile of saddlery, organising what looked like a major cavalry campaign, with sutures, syringes, bandages, whipping cord, needles, blood transfusion things, little boxes of gut-rot pills, water purification tablets: all the kind of stuff I wouldn't have bothered with. And she was babbling on about visas for Bulgaria, Romania, Hungary, and Czechoslovakia, and Poland, and what made me so sure I'd get into East Germany? And to tell you the truth, I'd only got a couple of visas because it's such a drag trying to get hold of them and there are a million things I'd rather do than write tedious letters off to dusty embassies asking about visas. Besides I didn't want to do any of this trip and had this secret plan of ringing Roger from Bulgaria to tell him it was all off. But I could hardly let on to Chumpie, could I?

So just to make a show of things I set about shoving the saddles into their bags, which was about as much fun as pushing calves back into cows, then burst all the citronella bottles and got so angry I felt like ditching the whole lot in the Windrush, going to get all my animals and pushing off back home, and to hell with the consequences.

Anyway, I won't bore you to death with any more of that, or what it was like hanging around at Heathrow in blazing sunshine waiting for a plane which I hoped had conked out somewhere, and wandering around trying to find Mr Popof.

'When he does turn up I expect he'll just pop-off the other end,' Chumpie said.

When he arrived he introduced himself straightaway, and once on the plane had the sense to sit with a friend, so sparing us the agony of having to talk.

Three and a half hours later we came barrelling in over the Balkans in a storm, landing with a big bounce in Sofia airport in pouring rain, got collected by Penko Dinev, a friend of Julian Popof's, in a rattling gas-propelled Moskovitch, were driven through gloomy backstreets, arriving some time later halfway up a mountain, at a small private hotel where the bog was reluctant and the washing arrangements shared.

But it did.

It did better than dinner in the local restaurant where we sat on chintz chairs in a room lit by a single dying neon light and where a grubby, bleary-eyed waiter appeared swaying about in front of us to announce that liver was off.

'Anything else?'

'Chicken.'

'Fine.'

When the liver arrived it was cold.

But the wine was good.

When we got outside, it was pitch black, still pelting with rain, so Penko drove us to our little hotel, off some back road somewhere above Sofia on the slopes of Mount Vitosha, which all felt like a trip from heaven to hell by way of Balkan Air.

The Official Spy

Once we'd arrived I felt differently about things. It had been such an effort getting there, the idea of reversing everything and doing it all backwards just to get home and back to normality seemed a bit pointless. I decided not to ring Roger but rather wait and see what we could make of it all. Somehow, the money I had would have to stretch.

Besides, I wasn't going to get on that aeroplane again. Not after that landing. No doubt the take-off would be worse and it'd be safer riding home anyway. So I thought, well, there's nothing else to do, temporarily forgot about Gonzo and Punch and Dolly and, with a big heave, got on with it.

Now the first impression I had of the Bulgarians was that they were a brown-eyed and black-haired people, a bit Latin, but, of course, Slav. Chumpie, on the other hand, thought they were fair haired, European, not Latin or Slav at all.

Their writing is Cyrillic which is illegible unless you're some sort of a swot, and so any sign, menu or anything that needs reading is unreadable. The language is impossible too unless you've spent half your life there. But we tried.

The first thing we learned to say was, 'Does it always rain at this time of year?'

We discovered it did. All day. Nevertheless, we were taken to Sofia by Penko and Julian Popof next morning, to the riding federation to have a look at these expensive horses.

We went through Sofia.

I'd been to a communist city before – to Moscow, also to look at horses – and what strikes you about a communist city is it's sort of bald-looking because it doesn't have any pizazz. Half the street lights don't work, all the cars are conked out, the shops look about as jolly as dungeons and it all gives you the impression of being really dead-beat: which it is. But in a funny way, because there are no advertising hoardings or glossy neon lights, it's refreshing. It's good to be able to look at a building uncluttered by posters. The snag is you quickly spot that this is no accident, but a design, and only when you wander into a shop to find it bare do you realise you've hit half a century of totalitarian oppression and it's a shock. There isn't anything to buy. Even if there was, there isn't the currency to buy it, and even if you had the currency to buy it, to get anything of any sort of quality, you have to go to the hard currency shop – foreign exchange shop, the dollar shop – and buy western goods at silly prices because most communist goods are dodgy. Accordingly, western goods have social cachet, and things like deodorants, bars of soap or empty bottles of whisky decorate cabinets like ornaments, because they imply that someone in that household has had access to western cash, and that has clout.

But in spite of the gloominess, old Sofia manages to be a grand city somehow, with wide traffic-free boulevards cobbled in honey-coloured brick, and lined with municipal buildings, colonnaded and tall. Here the domes of Aleksander Nevski Cathedral and the gold multi-onioned domes of the Russian Orthodox church are a blazing contrast to the boarded-up, potholed and ramshackle poured-concrete monsters on the outskirts of town, the nastiest reminder of communist flair at its architectural best, hurling up the kind of buildings it believes a good communist ought to make himself content in. And, if you are a good communist you'll probably be a party member and that means you'll get a house for being a good worker somewhere out in the country, which you can go to in your communist car, your Moskovitch, Skoda, Dacia or Lada, or your Trabant – small, two-stroke engined things that wheeze along all over the road, gassing the pedestrians. The biggest cars are Russian Zils, which you get if you're a real big shot in the party, and we saw a thundering cavalcade of these burning past, scattering Trabants like plates of sprats. We were told it was party officials going home for lunch.

When we were in the city, there was talk about elections, it sounded like things were going to change, communism was going to get the boot. It felt positive.

That's what it felt like. I was to discover the reality later – straight from the horse's mouth.

And it was a horse's mouth I was staring into at the riding federation when told one of the white Arabs – of which there were four – was eight years old.

'Eleven,' I said.

Mr Pesev, the boss, hoofed it. Maria, our translator, said he'd gone off to find out the horse's age. He came back and said the horse was nine and a half. I didn't look in the black horse's mouth. I was staring at the Arabs. I wouldn't have given 800 dollars for the lot.

Julian Popof and Penko were hanging about looking bored and it wasn't long before they left.

'Pop-off,' Chumpie said.

'What about village horses? Gypsy horses?' I asked. Maria tried it on Mr Pesev. He shrugged his shoulders. 'What about village horses?'

'Can't I buy village horses?'

'No. Village horses are no good. And anyway they have no papers and you can't export horses if you buy them in leva [the currency of Bulgaria] and you, as a foreigner, can't buy horses or anything from a villager with dollars.'

'Gypsy horses?'

'All gypsy horses are bad.'

Snookered.

And although I've never had much luck with them before, we made for the British Embassy, just in case someone could help, but we had to be quick because it was Friday.

Taxis are a cinch in Sofia, and since the exchange rate was good for tourists, the taxi we took was cheap. We rattled through the town, over tramlines where dilapidated old trams lurched and clattered about, we hurtled over cobbles, through streets of baroque peeling buildings worn out and grey behind budding trees.

When we got to the embassy we were let in and hung about for a while with a group of people trying to get visas for England when the vice-consul, Bob Gordon, introduced himself asking what he could do for us. We told him. He looked at his feet.

'I don't know where to get horses, but I can give you a bit of paper which will set you on your way,' he said and an hour later we were handed a document, written in Cyrillic, translated for our benefit, and that piece of paper was worth it. He set a precedent which was followed by all the other embassies and now I've got a collection of these letters which say I can ride horses all over everywhere, all because of Bob Gordon.

I told him we had permission from the Bulgarian authorities but hadn't, actually. All I'd done was mention the idea to Mr Popof who waved his arms around vaguely and said yes, yes, he'd see, and that was the extent of my enquiries. Sorry about that, Bob. But it seemed to do the trick, didn't it?

Bob's letter quoted what I told him, which was that the Bulgarian authorities had agreed. I didn't expand on it and nobody questioned me.

He added we should see Colonel Ivan Dimitrovitch Zvegintsov.

Colonel Ivan Dimitrovitch Zvegintsov?

I didn't want to: he'd ask questions. I wanted to avoid people who'd ask questions. Colonel Ivan Dimitrovitch Zvegintsov sounded like a man who didn't like woolly-headed ideas. I expected he could get us thrown out of the country. He was a big wheel, knocked about with all the top brass, was friends with all the generals and brigadiers and ministers. I didn't rate our chances with Colonel Ivan Dimitrovitch Zvegintsov, I didn't rate them at all. I didn't have any plans, no idea where we were going, didn't speak the lingo, only had a tourist map of the country and not the vaguest outline of a route.

'If you come down to the bar,' Bob said, 'at one o'clock since it's TGIF, there's a chance he might come down as well.'

'TGIF?'

'Thank God It's Friday.'

'Ah.' And Colonel Zvegintsov? In the bar? What? What was this Russian doing in the British Embassy bar?

He held out his hand.

'Zog Zvegintsov,' he said.

He was very direct.

'Zog: I'm the official spy. You're the horsey people I hear. I think I can help you.'

Colonel Ivan Dimitrovitch Zvegintsov, born in India, English public school, Oxford, Coldstream Guards, was the British Military

Attaché in Bulgaria at the time, and he and his wife Carrie set us on our way on horseback through some of the most lovely country I have ever ridden, and a bag of experiences I don't want to repeat.

Strawberry Roan

Over lunch, Zog told us a joke. He'd heard it from a Bulgarian general. He tried it on us: it goes like this.

Three people, a Russian, an Englishman and a Bulgarian were the only survivors of an aircraft that crashed onto a desert island.

They found themselves surrounded by cannibals.

One of the cannibals was more educated than the others, and stepped forward. Seeing three big dinners arrive in front of him, he reckoned two of them would do for the pot and the other could go free. He came up with an on-the-spot game.

'Aha!' he roared, 'I am a just and merciful man. Now if any of you have come from a country I have heard of, then I shall spare him!'

The Englishman pushed forward.

'Britain!' he exclaimed, 'I come from Britain! The Queen! Lords! Lloyds! All the pink on the map! The British Empire! Victoria! Rolls Royce! Cucumber sandwiches! Tea!'

The cannibal shook his head. The Englishman was tossed into the pot.

The Russian grinned. 'I am from Russia! From Moscow! Kirov! Lenin! Trotski! One fifth of the world's surface! And Tchaikovski! Dostoievski! Stalin! Vodka! Uri Gagarin! The Red Revolution!'

The cannibal shrugged his shoulders and the Russian joined the Englishman.

By this time the Bulgarian was walking toward the pot tearing off his clothes.

'Wait!' cried the cannibal, 'You have not had your turn! Speak!'

The Bulgarian continued tearing and carried on walking.

'Bulgaria ...' he mumbled.

'What was that? What was that?' the cannibal shouted, 'Bulgaria? Bulgaria? Sofia? That's where I went to university! It's where I read geography!'

'They're a great lot,' Zog said, 'Anyone who's got a sense of humour like that has to be. Get them on the subject of national heroes; they'll keep you in stitches for hours.'

Lunch ran to dinner and Zog related how he had been offered a T 34 Russian tank for a British museum. By the time dinner was over, the tank was pink, had a bunch of flowers up the barrel and Zog was driving it back to England. What with peace breaking out all over the place it seemed a marvellous plan.

'Of course you'll need a hell of a lot of political goodwill to go round chewing up tarmac with a T 34,' he said, 'but I daresay it could be swung.'

The pink and the flowers were Chumpie's embellishments. I'm not sure if Zog really took to them.

The next day, Chumpie and I left our little private hotel and moved in with him, saddles, bridles, girths and saddlebags. With us we brought the smell of mud and leather and then found out that Carrie – his wife – was allergic to horses. Even so, next day she drove us out on the plains surrounding Sofia to look at village ponies.

We went to a fair, where there were ducks, chickens, pigs, cattle and horses and the one I fell for because she was the prettiest colour I have ever seen was a beautiful 12-hand strawberry roan. If I'd had a truck I would have taken her there and then: as a child's pony she would have been wonderful: for us, she was too small. The others we looked at were passable, mostly bay, except one placid old chestnut mare whose hind legs were longer than her front ones.

'Fine,' Chumpie said. 'Good for going uphill.'

But we left her, despite it being uphill all the way to England, so Carrie reckoned. Then there was this argument about whether we should really take good horses from good homes. Was it right? Could we export them from Bulgaria if we bought them in leva? Could we buy them in leva? Were they the right price anyway at 5,000 leva each – about £375 pounds at the tourist rate? In any event, the price was a sight better than 5,000 dollars, and things started to look up.

It was during this time too we encountered our first dissident who came up to talk to us in the street one afternoon in Sofia and started waffling on about how polluted Sofia gets in hot weather because it lies in a basin. He asked us round to his house later on, which turned into a tense evening. I'd better not tell you the name of this man since there is still a state secret police force in Bulgaria, and he'd spent time in one of the labour camps. He showed us scars, told us stories of privation, of starvation. These labour camps were where dissidents were whipped off, and he had been in the worst, in Belene, an island on the Danube. He wasn't certain how many of these camps still existed at the time of our meeting but told us there were fifty before 10 November 1989, when Todor Zhivkov fell from power. Indeed, we came across election slogans which were little more than maps pointing out the whereabouts of each of these labour camps, and there are no prizes for which political party found mileage in that line.

As we sat with him, the television news came on. He translated for us. A few members of the communist party were standing outside a newly decorated church admiring the fresh paintwork. They were telling the camera that good communism included religion and how they had been responsible for keeping it alive for the past forty years. Our host just managed to prevent himself from shoving his boot through the screen before snatching the plug out of the wall and extinguishing any further viewing at a stroke. He went on to explain how the communists had thrown his father out of the house they were in, had stolen his business, that there had never been an ounce of compensation and that in order to try to keep the house they'd rented parts out and now lived in two poky rooms on the top floor. He hated communism with a passion, and like Zog, predicted their win at the June elections, because 'there are one million members of the communist party in this country and if you add all their families together then practically everyone is a communist or certainly influenced by someone in the family who is a direct agent.' He added that the Turks needed kicking out of Bulgaria, that Macedonia rightly belonged to Bulgaria as well as parts of Serbia, and that all land south of the Danube is also rightly theirs. Lastly, he thought the gypsies needed sterilising.

Then he told us a joke.

'Lateral thinking joke,' he said, with a wink. 'A trainload of young pioneers – that is communist elite youth – were on a train heading for Varna. Ten got off in Plovdiv, ten in Sofia, three in Velika Turnovo, twenty-one in Ruse, and twelve got on in Sumen. The question is, how old is the general secretary of the communist party?'

With that we left, dazed.

In the meantime we had still been keeping an active interest in developments at the riding federation and had actually put in a bid on the two Arab horses of 1,000 dollars apiece, which made me feel ill. That was two-thirds of my entire capital.

But our saddles fitted them: they fit any horse. I had been given them by Keith Bryan of Walsall to test. They're called 'Pathfinder' endurance saddles, and they really are the best long distance saddles I've come across. They've got a deep gullet, are well stuffed and they fitted the witherless Arabs equally well as fat village ponies – and I'm fussy about what saddle fits what horse. The headcollar bridles didn't fit the Arabs' small heads, so we would have to do something about them. And there was another problem.

I had had a running battle with the old codgers who fed the horses at the riding federation, who were shovelling oats down them, making them mad.

'No oats!' I cried, and they nodded. Now this was extremely confusing. In Bulgarian a nod accompanied by a '*ne*' means no. And a shaking of the head, what we understand to mean no, in Bulgarian means yes. So when I told the old boys to stop cramming oats into the horses and they nodded, I couldn't work out if they'd said yes or no, so said it again and they nodded again, and I was none the wiser.

That afternoon the horses were fed full rations: oats.

'No oats!' I cried again.

'*Ne!*' they chimed, nodding.

Next morning, all horses, full rations.

'If you give these horses oats again I will not buy them.'

'*Ne!*' they said, and nodded.

'They only need hay! They're impossible to handle! It's the oats! Oats have a funny drug in them which makes horses crazy!'

'*Da*,' they agreed shaking their heads.

Next afternoon, all horses, full rations.

Exasperating as it was, we attempted to ride the horses, two quite pretty Arabs, but the gelding was totally insane. The mare, whom we called Epsibar, was a sweet young filly, but had a bad rope burn on her offside hind leg and was impossible to shoe. Blood samples had been taken but not resolved, the whole thing was beginning to look so disorganised and the horses so dodgy, we finally chose to pull out of further dealings with the riding federation and, in a vague attempt to save face, bailed ourselves out with a sprinkling of dollars.

A day later we were sitting in the car with Carrie and her allergy to horses, on our way out once again to the villages.

'Talk about the blind leading the blind,' she murmured as we whisked through the gathering spring on the road to Kovachevski. Here the landscape was gullied and twisted, with red pantile roofed villages, where cows mooched about in the road and donkeys stood in harness beneath trees and blue denimed old men chatted over bundles of freshly cut lucerne. The road wound on up through the fringes of Vitosha National Park and we gazed down on villages crouching in valley bottoms, quarry brick coloured, a mixture of traditional housing and new concrete, sharp edged and formless.

In Kovachevski, Carrie pulled up, got out of the car and addressed the first pair of cow-smelling, grey-stubbled, podgy-blue pig-clutchers that shambled past. She was instantly surrounded. One of the pig-clutchers pulled a badge out of his pocket and yelled 'Margaret Tatcherrrr!!' and Carrie translated his tirades.

'They're all going to vote democratic in this village. No communists here,' and then one of the old boys led her away. She looked tiny in amongst all those gumboots and denim. Chumpie meanwhile got herself tied up photographing gypsies and Carrie disappeared, reappearing twenty minutes later out of breath.

'They thought I said icon,' she said puffing. 'I've been looking at icons.'

'Icons?'

'Icons. "*Ikon*" is "icon", and "*kon*" is horse. They couldn't believe I wanted to buy horses and thought I wanted icons.'

'What about the icons?' Chumpie enquired, wide eyed.

'Do you want to see?' Carrie was catching her breath.

Then another blue-denimed old man appeared from behind a clump of bushes, flagged us towards him and led us in silent procession across the street past decaying wattle and daub ultramarine blue barns into his yard. It was small. A playful puppy threw itself around, chickens, not unlike Exchequer Leghorns picked about in the manure heap: wood was neatly stacked in a pile by the doorway and an aged Mrs Blue Denim was spinning wool just inside what I took to be a kitchen.

We were all told to sit on the log in front of the dung heap, which we did, swatting flies. The old boy then disappeared into a shed, bringing out behind him a gentle lolloping old white-socked chestnut horse who looked as though he and the old man were part of one another.

'Well?' Carrie asked. I wondered if she was about to burst out in spots and rashes.

'Er ... yes ... but, he's only one, we need two.' The price was right. 3,000 leva: about £214. Carrie caught the old man's eye.

'*Due koni ... drug eta*?' She turned to us. 'I hope he isn't going to dig out more icons.'

He shook his head.

'Damn,' I thought.

'Right!' Carrie said and got up.

'What now?'

'He's got another,' she said. 'Didn't you see him shake his head?'

Further down the village we met another old fellow who showed us a bright young horse, but since we had neither saddles nor bridles nor anything with us, resolved to leave the whole thing and come back a few days later to try them and buy them, and so we all went back to Sofia, where I had a dreadful haircut, which together with an awful hat I bought on the cheap in Oxford made Chumpie remark that I looked like Benny Hill on holiday.

Dancing Bears

During the following few days we wandered about Sofia, and saw the gypsies and their dancing bears, which are at once a colourful and wretched sight. The gypsy wears bright clothing and with his bear on a short chain attaches him to his wrist, then plays a kind of one stringed violin and the bear rolls and writhes to the music. The bears are tethered by their necks or noses and the whole performance, though exotic, just left me feeling sorry for the bears.

The circus we gave a miss too. I can't cope with circuses.

But the gypsies themselves, the ones I saw in the market, the brightly dressed girls and their sun-brown children, they attracted me, and I found myself drawn to them and knew in time I should be amongst them, because secretly, in my heart, it was from the gypsies I intended to buy the horses. The gypsies were one of the reasons for my being there, yet I found myself afraid of meeting them face-to-face.

We had a look round the shops and met the mannerless old dragons who run them – why are they so sour? What is it about them? Is there a special school for learning how to be extra acidic to foreigners? There wasn't one store we visited where the woman behind the counter wasn't perfectly foul. No, they didn't have this, no, you couldn't see that, no, this part of the shop was shut, no, the lights don't work, no, there isn't any sugar, no, you can't go over there and look at that, no, the shop isn't open tomorrow morning.

The mosque was shut too, so was the Hammam, a nice old building made of white limestone and striped with bands of small bricks, with a grand arched doorway, decorated with relief tiling on a cherry background. It had trees growing out of the gutters.

Just as Chumpie was taking a photograph of Aleksander Nevski Cathedral a young fellow calling himself Lyudmil Spassov pitched up announcing he would be our 'free guide'. Eighty leva later I wondered about that, but he was nice, and seemed to know what he was talking about, so we took him on.

He told us all about Aleksander Nevski Cathedral, completed in 1912, which was built as a memorial church to the Russians for their part in the liberation of Bulgaria from the five-hundred-year-old 'Turkish yoke'– sometimes wrongly written with a 'j' spelling 'joke'.

The cathedral, for me, had no great style outside. Inside it was different, with its high domes – a peculiar reminder of the mosques it overthrew. The walls are marble, with small chapels standing on raised marble pedestals supporting smaller, more intricate domes, gilded, echoing the larger. Glorious candelabra hang from the high roof, lighting the icons, the paintings, the onyx, alabaster golds and bronzes.

A service was going on when we were inside, and the singing that heady Russian-like descant which makes the hair prickle on your neck.

Lyudmil chipped in: 'Aleksander Nevski was a great man, liberator of slaves and saved people from cruel torture from Turkishmen, and he was a noble. Then when he was old he was a greater man even and came to be holy and in the end was the biggest monkey in the church.'

I saw Chumpie bite her lip. I didn't know where to look: certainly not at her. I gazed into the dome, trying not to imagine Aleksander Nevski swinging about up there, in the chandeliers. Sometimes you can hold things together, sometimes not.

I had to get out.

It took a lot of explaining to Lyudmil, whom we appeased with a meal, a couple of bottles of wine, and a four and a half hour walk round Sofia, visiting every museum, every palace, park and dancing bear. Then he left us, he had to go home, vowing one day to marry a western woman so he could travel, and, no, he didn't want a Bulgarian wife because they didn't have international passports. He gave Chumpie a long look, disappeared down a darkening street and we returned to Carrie and Zog's flat.

Zog had in the meantime returned to England and his daughter Belle arrived, young, pretty, curvy and keen to go and look at horses, adding a fillip to our flagging spirits.

So it was with Carrie and Chumpie and Belle that I sat once more in the creamy sunshine in the tiny courtyard of the old blue-denimed man in Kovachevski. The day was warm and bright and reflected hard on the whitewashed walls; in dark shadows chickens and goats moved in shaded silence. The old lolloping white-socked chestnut was trying to eat my bridle. Both Chumpie and I had ridden him and found him such a docile old horse we couldn't imagine him fending for himself or having to think his way out of a tricky spot, which a travelling horse must be capable of. The horse was a no-goer.

We went to look at his friend's horse on whom I put the saddle, realising as I did he'd never been ridden. Unridden horses are no real problem; if you have to make them to the saddle, you have to make them and that's that. But there was something about this one. I saw it in his eye. There was no way I was going to get on him. But a gypsy did. And he did with the wrong foot in the stirrup and he, horse, saddle and all went screaming off out of sight, vanished over the horizon, and the horse came thundering back ten minutes later, riderless, boiling, pursued by a limping, jangling team of hobbled ponies, rattling in their chains, neighing and whinnying, and darted about by a bevy of kicking foals.

And so it was with Carrie, Chumpie and Belle I sat once more in the creamy sunshine in the tiny courtyard of the old blue-denimed man in Kovachevski, shook hands and pushed off.

We walked heads down through wattled and walled village backstreets, past the bent platinum-toothed old crones crabbing about, sprinkling corn grit to scratching, bare-bottomed bantams, past shuttered, sleepy houses to the car and drove back to Sofia. We drove in silence as the countryside flew past, the rolling blue distance and roadside juniper bushes, the line of poplars along a wandering stream and the mountain stood up high above us, pink in the setting sun.

'You should go to Samokov,' Carrie said. 'If you want to find gypsies, you'll find them there. And there's a horse fair.'

Once in Samokov I decided to aim for the gypsy quarter and found it.

Was it rough. It stank. It had exactly the same rotten smell about it I'd come across in Saudi Arabia years before when I found a herd of dead camels in the Nafud desert, the same dry, bitter rotten smell. A heaving pile of rubbish straddled half the entrance to the place where a pack of starved, flea-ridden dogs were pulling at a carcase. The houses were squalid little hovels with rags for doors, behind which snotty-nosed, naked children watched olive-eyed and suspicious of this pink tourist looking for a horse.

A crag-faced, gorilla-handed, furtive individual was my guide. And if he was the dirtiest bloke in town, if he stank, if he blew palls of dung-coloured smoke into my face, if he was rude, if he was all the worst things you can imagine, he was also the alivest bloke in town. He laughed and spat, slapped me on the back, roared at his companions, begged for money, took me to every dive he could, scolded me for being foreign, called me '*gaje*', called me '*chicho*'. Then he felt faint all of a sudden and didn't want to look for horses anymore, but twenty levas fixed that. Then he had a headache. Another twenty and it vanished. Then he was very weary and had to sit down and complained when I gave him another ten leva that it wasn't enough and so I gave him another ten, and he complained even louder.

He practically burst into tears when I left him and wrung my hand again and again, and beseeched me to buy his poor, worn, skeleton of a horse for 2,000 dollars. I, in turn, swore at him for treating his horse badly, made signs that he would go to hell if he was cruel to his horse, and when that made him pull faces, made signs that he would go to hell anyway, and he replied he was already there.

We parted friends and enemies because I refused to give him my watch and boots, and refused to spend all my money on a month-long bender with him.

Besides I wasn't in the mood, even though he was.

I saw him later that day, flat out under a willow. He had flies crawling in and out of his mouth.

He was called Jirim and what was important about him was that he put the word about.

Gypsy Horse

Jirim told me about The Italian.

I know about The Italian. He goes round Europe buying horses and sends them to Italy for salami. He sends them in big trucks and they go all that way without food or water. Those trucks run from Russia to Italy, Poland to Italy, Czechoslovakia, Hungary, Romania, Bulgaria – all for salami. All the native horses and ponies are disappearing for salami.

Jirim said if I didn't buy his horse he'd sell him to The Italian.

If I bought Jirim's broken-down grey, I knew what he'd think. He'd think he could sell any old mule to any sucker for any price, and never bother to feed his horse again.

I turned him down, and told him I only bought good horses for good money so it would be in his best interest to look after his if he wanted to sell it.

I told him what I thought of him after that and I told him what I thought of The Italian.

Then there was Zhivko. Zhivko had a taxi business and lived in Samokov. He knew most things about the place and said he thought he could help.

Zhivko spoke a bit of English and took us round all the nags in Samokov, screeching to a halt each time we saw a likely one on the road. We even wound up trying to buy an old grey from a butcher who was unloading meat from the wagon into a cold store.

We looked at more pink horses, black stallions, horses fifty kilometres away, we looked in farm yards, backstreets, uptown, downtown in the gypsy quarter and then, one overcast morning, the fair.

I saw Little Pink standing in harness in the shafts of a yellow cart with his head down, under some willow trees. He was maybe 15hh, strawberry roan with a double mane, and he had clean legs, good quarters, a good back and no sores. The gypsy led him out of the shafts with gleaming eyes: here was the tourist with the dollars. A crowd gathered. This was an unridden horse: he'd have to be made. Poor little sod was only three years old but I said I'd buy him for 3,800 leva, knowing damn well that the chances of exporting him were nil, that the horse could well be someone else's, that he was head-shy, which meant he'd been hit about, that he'd never been out of harness and that he was probably a brute to handle.

I said I'd pay in the morning and that I wanted the horse shod and outside the cafe near the old mosque in Samokov, at eight. Then Little Pink was jammed back into his cart, the gypsy took hold of the reins and he whipped that horse from a dead stop to a gallop and whipped him all the way down the road. If I'd had a rifle then I think I'd have shot that man.

But that was one horse down and I needed another. Chumpie was with Zhivko a little distance off. I could see the look on Zhivko's face. He disapproved of me buying horses from gypsies, and so did his father, a difficult old man with a pained expression. He definitely thought I was an imbecile, didn't know what I was doing, should have kept looking, bought horses from the Bulgarians not the Turkish *tsigani*. He shook his head. He was sure I didn't know what I was doing. Then up went a shout and the crowd parted. Another gypsy came into the ring riding bareback on a black horse, a biggish black horse, big that is, for a gypsy horse: maybe 14.2hh, 14.3 at a push. The horse had a big head, long body, and uneven feet. He was very poorly shod. The gypsy slipped off. Zhivko handed me a saddle and up I got. The horse was tattooed with a number: 316. Which gypsies tattoo horses? This had to be a stolen horse.

'Is this a stolen horse?'

Zhivko repeated my question. I rode off from the row that caused.

This horse was a bulldozer with a mouth to match. He didn't care much where he put his feet either but he was solid. I reckoned if he'd survived gypsy handling he had to be good, and something told me he was good, even if he didn't care where he put his feet. He hadn't long been castrated either and had septic sores, but I had stuff for things like that. The horse was six years old and had a rope burn on his offside hind.

The haggle didn't last long.

Eight o'clock next morning, same place as Little Pink.

'Karo!' The gypsy shouted to Chumpie and ripped a handful of hairs from his mane then handed them over.

The horse was hers.

At eight on the nail the following day we were at the cafe near the old mosque with the two gypsies and the two horses. Karo, the black horse, looked well enough but the other one had a filthy job of shoeing done to him. Poor little beggar had his feet nailed up with a set of stilettos and where the hoof spread over the shoe, they'd just whacked it off with a hammer. That horse couldn't straighten his legs. I bought him anyway and gave the man his money, which he took, got into Zhivko's taxi and the counting started. They counted the money twice, then he got out and gripped my hand. I don't know what he said but it sounded friendly enough. He gave the horse a pat as he pushed off without looking back, and he and a bunch of his cronies swaggered away like they'd just pulled off the biggest deal in history. He ripped me off on his terms but I can live with paying 400 dollars for a decent young horse, even if his feet were smacked about. Then it was the other fellow's turn and, once again, in the taxi with Zhivko for the counting. He tried it on once saying I had to pay more but I told him he'd either take the money or the sale was off. He took the money. Then we had to register the horses in some dusty little office with some dusty little bureaucrat and Zhivko did all the talking.

So there we were, surrounded by a crowd of people, standing in the middle of Samokov, hanging onto what any English horse coper would regard as a pair of pretty indifferent jades.

Zhivko told us to take them to Drugsheenovo, a little village to the west of town, where his old man had a place, and we could clean them up a bit because they both stank to high heaven. By the end of the day we'd groomed them, washed them, cut their tails and I cut the stilettos off Little Pink.

We tried to think of other names for Little Pink: Parsifal, Zhivko, Stotinki or Nevski or something but nothing stuck. He was going to be Little Pink, and that's what we called him.

Later in the afternoon we took them both out for a graze on long tethers and I reckon that was the first time Little Pink had tasted meadow grass. I reckon too it was the first time he'd been out of town without a cart behind him, and the first time he'd been allowed to kick and roll and mess about like any young horse and I saw him stretch and whinny like the world was shining and new.

It only took twenty minutes to make him to the saddle. He bucked a couple of times, but as soon as he knew I wasn't going to hit him for no reason he eased into the bit and settled down. Chumpie rode Karo, who looked steady enough but you could see if he wanted to go he wasn't going to let that little snaffle stop him. He was a strong horse, Karo, and no mistake. She did well to ride him up that hill that afternoon, and she did well to hang on when a bunch of yapping sheepdogs came belting up behind her and tried to spook the horse, but she calmed him down, and he didn't flinch.

While all this was going on we'd been staying in the old monastery in Samokov, which was a pretty old place, but they didn't stamp this *carte statistiqui* thing you're supposed to carry around with you and get stamped every night. It could mean you got in trouble trying to get out of the country if the *carte statistiqui* wasn't up to date, but we'd fudged the thing up so much anyway, we gave up with them. By the time I reached the frontier I'd lost mine anyway.

This monastery actually was a convent and run by a covey of ageing nuns and they didn't know about *cartes statistiquis* and moithered about pulling up weeds. And wasn't that a noisy place? If there wasn't somebody wandering around ringing bells, there was somebody wandering around beating sticks, then there was singing, or a wedding, or communion, or these cats caterwauling or all the doors slamming and nuns shouting. So we were both pretty glad to get away, despite it being a sight better than the big touristy hotel up in Borovets which was one of these big ski resorts, which you can keep.

We got away on a Wednesday morning after packing the horses with all the gear. You wouldn't believe how quiet they were. Even though the old man shoved a pile of oats down them, they were still quiet. Little Pink surprised me because I was certain he was going to try to buck all those bags off, but he didn't, and old Karo behaved as though he'd been covered in bags all his life. Each horse had a saddle, pommel panniers, saddlebags, bedroll, ground sheet, thick numnah and long tether line and the whole issue must have weighed forty pounds; perhaps a touch more. And though we rode those horses for mile on mile they never once got a rubbed back, nor did we ever get them sore.

So when the horses were loaded, the old man and Zhivko and all were going to see us off. The idea was the old man would point out the way over the mountain, the way to lhtiman. He was going to come along with his pushbike, doing his kind of soft whistle all the time.

The old man was called Mitko and he wore a navy blue beret squashed down on his head with his old white hair sticking out. He had pale horn-rimmed specs, and a pale blue denim jacket, and one cycle clip. He was a good-looking old man but he was touchy.

Golden Orioles

It felt good to have the horses, smell them, hear the creak of the leather, and see their feet push into the soft red earth. Old Mitko pumped away on his bike weaving about the track and there was Zhivko standing behind waving, and shouting, *'Pryaten Put!'* wishing us a good trip. We waved until he fell from sight.

Round us the fields were green and the willows by the stream silvery. And it was dead quiet: except for old Mitko and that funny whistle of his, and the clank his bike made every time the wheel turned and caught the mudguard. In the distance a golden oriole hooped away in the trees and I heard those birds for the next two thousand kilometres but I only saw one once.

Every now and then you'd see a little herd of cows grazing with their herders lying about in the grass either half-cut or half asleep and they'd eye us as we went by then roll over and doze again in the sun.

A few kilometres later the old man was heaving his breath out pushing that bike of his through mud in a lot of pine trees when he stopped. He was knackered. He laid the thing down and started gasping on about which way we should go because he'd had enough of showing us the way and now it was up to us. He spoke slowly and repeated everything, pointing here, there and everywhere but he might as well have said it all in Javanese because neither of us understood a word he said. It didn't matter much though and we headed off the way we thought he said which took us high into the hill and on to a wide dirt track and when we got there we heard the old boy yelling his head off because we'd gone wrong and so up he came puffing like a train, pushing that bike and shoving his deaf-aid into his ear and roared at us pointing out the way again and stomped away cheesed off, but he turned around, smiled and waved.

I liked old Mitko, even though he was touchy.

So we were on our own. I thought of Ahmed Paşa, the old stallion I rode through Turkey. His story is told in *Saddletramp*. How it all reminded me of him and those big mountains north of Denizli. He was a good old horse, Ahmed Paşa. And Little Pink did exactly what he did, gazing about him as though he'd never heard of any of this stuff before, as though he'd never seen trees or a forest or been high on a mountain and felt the wind in his mane. He was like that because he hadn't. I know he hadn't. It was new to him and he reacted to it. He wanted to see round the next corner, look round the next tree and he felt free, I know he did. He'd have spent his life in Samokov, that young horse, born in some filthy stable and when big enough he'd have joined his mother in harness, tied to her with a bit of string and trotted round town all day, in the cold and the heat and that's all he would have known until he was big enough to pull the cart himself and his mother died or got killed, or was taken away or sold and he would have been left to work alone. But now here he was with Karo who was doing the same.

I reckoned Karo knew a bit more because I was sure he was a pinched horse from Pleven, so he would have had to have been brought to Samokov from Pleven somehow and maybe he'd legged it once already. Maybe he went in a truck, there's no telling; or maybe it was just his age and he was that bit more mature. All the same he gawped about like someone who'd just been set free after a few years in prison. They were great those horses that day. And when we stopped two or three hours later for a break, Karo put his head down and ate while Little Pink cavorted about too excited to eat. Really, Little Pink was much too young, not physically, because he was strong, but he was immature mentally and it showed. All the same, it's a good feeling to have a young horse and take him off the streets and introduce him to a world he has the right to live in.

That afternoon it poured. But just before the lightning got going an old shepherd came past with his sheep, stood up on the hill and played his flute, and that reminded me of Turkey too. We watched him. The music was repetitive but it stuck in your head: Little People music, reedy and weird. He had one goat with his sheep. The reason he had a goat is because it doubles the intelligence of the flock. They do it all over the eastern countries. He watched us for a bit, stayed a while longer then drifted off with his goat and his sheep and we had a bite of lunch, trying out a lump of pork fat Zhivko had given us. It must have weighed ten pounds, neat fat. We ditched it. Only later we discovered we'd slung away an expensive delicacy.

Our first night's stop was in Novo Celo where we fell into the hands of the village drunks. The horses wound up in a collective and we wound up back in Samokov in one of those hellish high rise blocks with a dipso, his sour cousin and a drum majorette daughter who treated us as though we were invisible. We were glad to be away next day out on the trail for Ihtiman, travelling.

Now the thing about travelling with horses is that a lot of it is no more than a slog. You get going in the morning, you stop to graze the horses, then you get going again in the afternoon and start to get worried round about five or six because you haven't found anywhere to stay and maybe it looks like rain. Some people plan their routes first, going along organising stopovers, but I don't like it that way and can't see the point in doing it if you know where you're going to be. I like going blind. I like it because it's full of surprises and you get sucked up into a country fast. And the thing about Bulgaria was that we were in places where they'd never heard a foreign voice nor met foreigners nor had actually been allowed to speak to them. We were objects of interest in a sense, though I don't want to make too much of that.

And so we went along on luck and chance and the compass, and that's what I like best, but it's a slog. And what often makes it a slog is that although you've got a map, you can't tell anything from a map. They're not much use. Certainly you get a picture of where you're heading, but you can't tell if someone has built some great concrete drainage channel right across your path, and you can't tell if the river they've marked is swimmable or not swimmable, if it's full of sewage or drinkable. And you can't tell if the village is going to be friendly with people who are willing to help or unfriendly. You can't tell if the woods are thick or passable, if the dirt tracks are clay or sand – in other words, all the things you need to know, you can't get from a map so I don't think much of them. I prefer my compass and trust my eyes and the horse's feet and that's the way we go, but it's a long way. Sometimes you get to short-cut everything, but mostly, you go long.

And it's not much use asking people the way because unless they've been that way with a horse, then the chances are they don't know. I can't say how many times I've asked a fellow the way only to find him wrong not a hundred yards from where he directed us. Old Mitko was right though: he looked like the kind of bloke who is right, and you can trust him, and besides, he was an old horse coper himself and the chances were the way he pointed out to us he knew like the back of his hand because he'd ridden it a hundred years ago when he was young.

And the other thing is, the horses get to know the routine. They get to know you pack them in the morning then you set off riding them and they get excited when it's time for their grazing and they can't wait for lunchtime and they can be funny then because they think it's lunchtime when it isn't, and keep trying it on. Or when you stop to look at the compass, or check out you're going the best way, they put their heads down because they hope you're going to chuck it in early that day because it's hot or something and they can roll and drink and eat then doze in the sun.

And then after lunch they act like a couple of blokes with big hangovers and it takes a long time to get any pace into them, but by five they're looking just as hard as you are for somewhere to stay, and very often they find it before you because they smell other horses and you follow the way they're scenting and you arrive in some beaten-up bit of a place where there's some crippled old man poking his pig about and he breaks into a smile because he's got horses too; he knows what you want and he's your friend. So you get to trust your horse and he trusts you and you get to like the old gaffers and their pigs and their raki.

I remember Ihtiman too. I remember the poster on the wall in Ihtiman, a cartoon of a big thick guy holding a shovel looking down on to a little clever guy holding a pile of books, and the little one was wearing specs – a cartoon intellectual – and the caption read ' I'll think – you work.'

We saw other banners too, the CDC slogans, the democratic party, and BCNP, the agrarian party, who, by and large, had a grip of the rural areas. The idea of an election was strange to most people, of actually having a voice, unheard-of, and so no one really believed it. They didn't believe they'd ever really get a chance and reckoned the communists would rig the whole thing and get back in again. After all, too many reds stood to lose and they were hardly likely to give in without a scrap. So if you got to talk to and understand someone, they weren't that taken with the idea at all. The commies always got their way, fair or foul. So they were apathetic. They'd had communism up to their ears, but they'd known it for forty years and everyone had his place and some kind of a job, and everyone knew the status quo. What worried the older generation was that they didn't want to change because there they were economising parasitically on chickens and pigs, they grew their vegetables in their patch, had a job in the collective and life was peaceful, even if it lacked any incentive or chance of improvement. So there was this sprawling grey communist town with its people sensing they were about to be cheated again. We didn't stay.

We cleared Ihtiman in the afternoon and wound up that night beside a river, which was sterile, dead, which is another communist trick.

All the same it was a soft place and the two horses were tethered on their long lines and Little Pink couldn't get over it and kept rushing around. There was a hermit of a man there too and he hobbled the horses while we were trying to find water to drink. Karo was dumbfounded. The hobbles completely snookered him and he didn't know what to do, but they didn't snooker Little Pink and he was as nimble with those hobbles as he was without them and didn't he show off. He leaped about the place, here and there, and old Karo was riddled with confusion, watching him, trying to make out how he did it and he went on and on doing it, showing off to Karo that he was a gypsy horse and knew all these kinds of tricks, but old Karo didn't, which made me certain he was a pinched horse from Pleven.

Then darkness fell and Chumpie and I lay out the groundsheets and our sleeping bags and I took the hobbles off the horses, who quietened down to graze, and the old hermit took his cattle into a little corral. He brought a bowl of yoghurt over later which I drank. A line of cow dung swum off his thumb into the yoghurt as he handed it over. He was a pretty filthy, but a nice bald old man. Chumpie and I lay down as the fireflies glided about, bats rasped the night sky, and we slept beneath the cow-belling moon as the river rolled past dark beneath the trees.

The Reservoir

There was an old gypsy with a head like an eagle. He had a big hooked nose and these scowling hooded eyes, his hands were like claws and he was tall and thin. Really, he looked like a half-starved old eagle with no energy left. He lives in Muhovo and Muhovo is a village right on a big reservoir. It's a kind of a no-hope place. When we got there we were nearly dead from thirst, and when we asked this old worn-out eagle for water, he said '*nyama*' – there isn't any. You get to hear '*nyama*' a lot in Bulgana.

But how could there be people there if there wasn't any water? There was this huge great reservoir wasn't there? What was it full of if it wasn't water?

'Industrial' comes the answer. Chemicals. So there were all these people and the big old gypsy with the eagle's head living by a reservoir unable to drink it. No anger: no blame: no cursing: just resignation: accepting it as if it was the most normal thing in the world. The reservoir had been polluted for so long they never even thought of it as a reservoir, just a big lagoon full of chemicals. There was nothing they could do. And if you tried to say they could do something if they changed the government, no one was interested in that line because they said no one can change the government because the government's a pile of commies and commies always get their way.

We found a tap though. The tap. The one the whole village drinks from. We were there in May, and they had all the summer to go through.

We tethered the horses in a field full of foxtail and went to a big concrete place with filthy net curtains and formica tables, a concrete floor and steel chairs. A Klondike space heater had a stove-pipe struggling out of it which cobwebbed its way across the room and over the serving hatch were decade-old Christmas decorations. There wasn't any electricity, no water and nothing to eat.

'*Nyama*', they said. We sat down anyway and I ordered a bottle of wine because we could see that, and about half an hour later we got cold pork chops with cold chips. And the old eagle just sat in the corner working his way through glasses of white wine and packets of cigarettes. He just sat there, staring off into the dirty curtains, sucking away at those cigarettes and swigging the wine and nobody talked to him.

Kondoms and Oboriste

It's fine travelling around Bulgaria on horses if it isn't raining because you can sing along looking at the shrikes and hoopoes and linnets and jays and things of which there are a great many, because unlike the Italians, Bulgarians do not regard them as pie-fillers. And when it's sunny you can take in the vetches, scabious and colours of the wild flowers, the big fields of crops, triticale, wheat, maize, sunflowers and rape. And it's fine travelling around on horses even if it is raining if you've got the kit to keep you dry so you can still look at all these things.

But if you haven't got the kit to keep you dry, it's not so fine. The kit we had kept you wetter than if you went along stark naked in a monsoon.

It did it like this.

We had capes which doubled as groundsheets and they were army ones. Ponchos. I don't know what kind of material they were made of but it did two things. First of all it frightened the horses, and secondly it let the wet in.

Then when it had done that it did another two things. It kept the wet in and then made you sweat, so not only did you get wet from the outside but you got wet from the inside as well and then when you were really drenched, it had a final trick, which was to freeze you.

I'm glad I'm not in the army.

We wore the things the day after we'd been dying of thirst in Muhovo because it slashed with rain all the way to Oboriste except for a couple of hours when it boiled. We kept the capes on then to dry them out a bit, and that was when we found out about the sweat. So we took them off, which was when we found out about how they scared the horses, and trying to ride a wet horse with an army cape wrapped round your head while he goes tearing off through a crop of wet wheat is not easy.

We should have thrown the capes away, but didn't have anything else, although thinking about it, they were worse than anything else, even being stark naked, and if you wonder why we kept them, I just couldn't tell you.

So there we were going along to Oboriste through all this gorgeous rolling countryside, steaming. Then just before we got to Oboriste this yellow cart came clattering towards us with a couple in it

'Avustralian!' the man was roaring, 'Avustralian!', and whipped his pony into a smart trot while his big Mrs wobbled about beside him clutching a bottle of green stuff they'd been sharing. He ran that pony into the ditch, then jumped off throwing his arms wide, still shouting 'Avustralian!' and then leaned over the cart, removed a cloth and revealed a load of honeycomb.

We were in a long field of oil seed rape which was in flower. Now I get nervous of honeycomb when it's not in the hive, and nervous of it when I'm on a horse, and even more nervous when I'm talking to a guy who's prodding about at a hive with a lot of the green stuff in him.

'Avustralian!' he bawled again winkling a frame of honey out, then came towards us. By this time I'd got off my pony, who was taking a big interest in this guy and his honeycomb, while Chumpie was having a hard time hanging on to Karo who was taking a big interest in the guy's pony, who seemed pretty keen to meet Karo and whom the lady with the bottle of green stuff was wrestling with, trying to keep him in the ditch. So we had a lot of hanging on to contend with and here was this guy plunging a knife into the comb and honey was oozing out all over the place, and I was looking around waiting for the bees to hit and all the time he was banging on about Avustralia.

He offered me a plug of comb on the end of a knife, which I took and that's when I found out about Little Pink and honey – I've never known a horse eat honey, but that one did. So this guy thought it was all a bit of a joke and scraped a dollop of honey into my hand for me to share with my pony, and none of that was easy.

'Course, this guy was out of his box. I don't know what the green stuff was, but it had got to him. His Mrs offered Chumpie a swig at the same time as he offered her a lump of comb and she had both hands hanging on to Karo. Little Pink was pulling faces and nodding the way horses do when they've got a mouthful of something they're not sure of and I was trying to wipe the stickiness off my hands in the grass when Chumpie floored us all by suddenly asking for a condom.

'Condom?' she said to this guy and pointed off down the road.

Well it stopped him dead: froze him. Stopped us all dead: what did she want with a condom? The guy was completely outflanked, with his dollop of honey dribbling off his knife and this strange foreign girl asking him about condoms from the back of a black pony right out in the middle of nowhere. He peered hard at her, then me, then his Mrs, then took a bite of his honey.

'Ha?' he asked with a mouthful of comb, and she said it again. His old Mrs shrugged her shoulders and they looked at one another frowning like they were trying to win some sort of frowning contest or like the girl had lost her marbles or was mad or something. I was stunned too. Condom? What did she mean? There? Then? Hadn't we got enough going on already? I looked down the road.

'Condom?'

'No, no,' Chumpie said. 'Stand still Karo ... stand still ... no, no, cond-dom,' and then pointed to Little Pink, the guy's pony and Karo, and down the road again. 'Oboriste kon-dom.'

The guy looked down the road, trying to get hold of this one but it was beyond him, so he patted his trouser pockets to show he didn't have any condoms or whatever she wanted. And that was when the old woman started this hacking laugh and jabbered something at the man, who picked it up and he too began to laugh, took the bottle off her, had a long swig and offered it to me, and I seemed to be the only one who was missing the point. I couldn't tell you what the green stuff in that bottle was either but it lifted the top of your head off.

'Look,' Chumpie said, 'not condom, kon-dom.'

I had another swig. What the hell was she talking about? Then I twigged. *'Kon'* is Bulgarian for horse, and *'dom'* is Bulgarian for house.

'Ah, not condom ... Kon-Dom!'

'Yes!' she said.

Horse-house! That was it. Did this guy know about a horsehouse in Oboriste? A place for us to stay for the night! I took it up: had he got a kon-dom?

He was rolling about clutching his belly either from the green stuff or the kon-dom and nodding which meant he hadn't got a kon-dom, then his Mrs was nodding, pointing off the other way saying, we guessed, their kon-dom was the way we'd come, and with that he gave me the frame of dribbling honey, got back into his cart, flipped the reins and went clattering off with the pony as Karo whinnied his head off and Little Pink tried to swipe the honey and I was looking about for bees wondering when they'd hit us and Chumpie was trying to take a photograph.

It rained again on the way to Oboriste and I can promise you one thing, and this is for sure. Never try to put a wet army poncho on when you're riding a three-year-old while you're hanging on to a frame of honey.

A Peculiar Theft

The old woman who put us up in Oboriste was called Stoyana and she was intelligent. She didn't have a kon-dom that wasn't already full of a kon but had another place where we could keep the horses for the night. Her father was ancient, but also intelligent and rigged up jackets for the horses, kind of Bulgarian/New Zealand rugs, then produced a pile of hay and lucerne.

He also gave them triticale and oats, another variation on their diet, which did them nothing but good. I never give my horses the same fare two days or even two meals running and have never had a sick horse as a result. I like variety, and so do the horses: lots of fruit if I can find it, which I mix with lucerne, and hard feed, maize, barley, oats or triticale, which is a wheat but doesn't blow like durum. I wouldn't feed the soft wheat you get in England.

And I believe that so long as the horse is kept walking, so long as you do thirty or forty kilometres a day, it doesn't matter what you give them, it can be as varied as you like, provided it's clean and you keep them grazing. It has been my experience that a travelling horse eats a tremendous amount of food and has to do so, not simply to keep him going in body, but also to nourish his soul, because eating and grazing is to a horse what suckling is to a lamb: it's a comfort, like whisky to a Scotsman. A travelling horse has to put up with a lot of stress because he hasn't got a home to go to and horses like to have a home, so you have to account for this and if you pile enough grub down them, then they'll stay pretty chipper. And, if you want them to last, you have to mother them along till they shine like liquid gold, and I always aim to improve the condition of a horse.

There was one problem with Little Pink though and that was he was so excited about everything he wasn't a good eater. He spent his whole time running about staring at everything and behaving like a baby, which meant the only way I could keep him in condition was to tether him short and he hated that. He hated it if he was tethered short and Karo was tethered long, but Karo was a good eater and took his food very seriously. Karo was the only horse I have ever known who can eat non-stop all day and all night. It's a good quality in a travelling horse. He must put his head down to eat every time you stop, because that's his petrol. But Little Pink just ran around and it was the devil trying to get grub down him. Nevertheless, in Oboriste when the old man gave them all this grub, the hay and lucerne from the collective, triticale and oats, then turned up with a bucket of apples, he had my thanks and that of the horses, and they both ate. Horses know damn well when you're looking after them and when you're not, and have a way of showing gratitude.

We were the first foreigners Stoyana had ever met, and she must have been about sixty. At first she was intrigued by us, especially by Chumpie who took an interest in all her handiwork, the lacework, embroideries and stuff while I was outside fiddling around with horse food. But Stoyana wasn't too sure whether we were allowed to stay with her or not so she took us off to the kmet, the mayor, to register.

It caused confusion.

The *kmet*'s secretary wrote down everything old Stoyana said, but when we handed over our passports, which he couldn't read because they weren't in Cyrillic, he got in a spin and it looked like we'd gone and done the wrong thing and should have kept them.

We were shown into the *kmet*'s office.

The *kmet* was a big man in a nylon shirt and brown shiny trousers. He looked like a bouncer. His mate, the second *kmet*, had a round face, and he also looked like a bouncer. They'd been sharing a joke when we walked in and tightened up on seeing us. The hard face the *kmet* put on everything told me the whole trip was about to be ended. I gave him Bob Gordon's letter. He took it, scanning the page. The room fell silent. He frowned. Was he going to have us bunged in choky? It seemed to take him forever to read. When was he going to finish the thing? His face bore no expression at all. Then he put the letter down and burst out laughing.

What was the old woman doing with these two *Anglichanin*? What was she going to do with the horses? And no, she couldn't charge for us, no, it wasn't a hotel, yes, she had to look after us, feed us, see to the horses. Stamp the *carte statistiqui*? There? In Oboriste? What with? No, do it in Panaguriste tomorrow. He'd telephone them, say we were coming, now bugger off and don't pester him again.

'*Sitchko-b'vo!*' he shouted as we left.

Back at Stoyana's place, she showed us to a warm room, and fed us the best meal we'd had in rural Bulgaria, which proved to me the point of going along blind. You just don't know what's going to happen and that's what makes it worthwhile.

The next thing that happened wasn't so good.

We were staying in a hotel and the horses were staying in a graveyard. I moved them from there to the marble cutter's place right round the back of Panaguriste where I fell in with a pile of hard drinking men and got fed pork fat and raki all afternoon until no one could speak and we all staggered back to where we'd come from with blinding headaches.

Karo and Little Pink I put in an open-fronted barn leaving them on their long tethers. This meant they could graze and get under cover if it rained. It seemed safe enough, particularly since there was a night guard who said he'd keep an eye on them.

We'd been warned the gypsies planned to steal the horses. Certainly when we arrived in town from Oboriste we were surrounded by a crowd, most of whom were gypsies. Both Karo and Little Pink at this stage were looking good. We were feeding them well, we groomed them and they were getting fitter. Their coats shone, their tails were cut level, manes combed, feet picked out and I'd done the best job I could with a lousy pile of shoeing. None of the gypsy horses were ever in good order. They were always poor, always mistreated and always filthy. And if there's one big criticism I have of the gypsies of south Eastern Europe, it is that for all their colour and vivacity, I thought them rotten horse copers. They didn't have a clue about horses. They couldn't handle them, most were scared of them, they always whipped them, they never fed them, and the horses were, as a result, always covered in sores. To this I'll add another thing, which is hard, and it's this: that gypsies have a special knack with horses is a myth. A myth they must have invented themselves. I've yet to come across a gypsy in Europe who knows how to handle a horse at all. The absence of the smallest degree of compassion left me often hating the gypsies and I thought they got the treatment they deserved.

The threat of theft by the gypsies was an ever-present one in Eastern Europe and when I was to cross the Danube, the threat increased. 'You can't go to Romania,' people said. 'It's too dangerous on horseback: you will be robbed and everything stolen.' Everyone said that – even the gypsies themselves.

That night in Panaguriste came a knock on our door. There was trouble. One of the horses had been stolen.

Theft is a miserable thing.

I felt sick when I heard that news. I reckoned it would be Karo. He was the one they always surrounded. He was the bigger horse, and they liked black horses.

Twenty minutes later, in drizzle, we were up with the horses who were both still there, except Karo was free. Just his headcollar and tether rope had gone. Who does a thing like that? Why pinch a headcollar and not the horse? The other explanation was that he'd been pinched altogether but had slipped his headcollar and come back to Little Pink.

Anyway, we shifted them to a Ivan Pavlov's stable and they spent the rest of the night there, but it all left me wondering and I came to the conclusion that whoever took that head-collar and rope was no gypsy. There was more to it than that. Chumpie had been told in the afternoon the marble cutters were no good. The marble cutters told me the people in the hotel were no good. And if you ask me, I don't reckon any of them were any good and the horses would have been safer with the gypsies.

In the morning we were confronted with having to sort out a new bridle arrangement for Karo using string and leather straps because being a headcollar bridle, what was missing was the whole doings and all we had were the reins and bit. But we fixed it all up and then along came a singing dark-eyed young fellow riding a little grey pony. He introduced himself as Slava and told us he was going to be our guide across the mountains to Koprivshtitsa. His pony was called Petko, who was wearing a kind of a saddle arrangement over a colourful but dirty saddlecloth. Where they both appeared from God only knows, but we followed them right out of Panaguriste, which was a long ride, but one of the loveliest I remember.

In rolling country, led by Slava, we rode high up into the mountain, following a stream. We saw red squirrels and deer and the air was blown with the smell of pine and fields were green with triticale. Higher again we found ourselves in grassland, thick with wild flowers, an embroidery of colours marvellous in variety and broken by tall rocky outcrops.

We passed low white-walled collective farms, abandoned and silent, their corrals rotted, all broken down. Away on a bank a shepherd waved, Slava hollered and a voice hollered back. Then the landscape changed into deep sandy gulleys, where juniper shrubs grew.

Way below us, red roofed in the valley, lay Koprivshtitsa and the mountains beyond.

It was a place I was dreading. I was dreading it because Chumpie was going back to England and I was to go on alone. But what was worse was that I was going to go on alone with one horse.

We got down to the place round about nightfall. Slava picked up a handful of dollars for his pains, then sorted the horses out a night's bedding in a gloomy old collective, thick with black cobwebs and a Dickensian workhouse atmosphere. He was funny, Slava, and all the way kept on pointing out mounds and things, saying it was the Levski route. 'Ak! Ak! Ak!' he'd shout, pointing at a tumulus, this, one of those moments when the prison of incomprehensive is dark indeed. Sitting sideways in his saddle he'd turn to watch us like we were a pair of fat wooden dummies on fat wooden horses, not thin and scrawny like his poor little pony, who looked as though he could use a few square meals all in one go. Then Slava would start up about Levski, the Bulgarian national hero, and why hadn't we sent our baggage on by taxi so we could gallop the whole way and stop taking up all his time.

All the same, that was a straight ten-hour ride, which is something I never do, and won't press the horses to do more than two and a half hours at once, and that way, they last, you don't get sores, no one gets bored and you keep going, a little at a time, and have a good time.

Farewell to a Friend

I could write about Koprivshtitsa and tell you how pretty a town it is, that it's a national revival place, that it's full of old buildings, that it has cobbled streets and is small and compact and cool and has quite a tourist trade. I could go on with these descriptions for page after page because I have plenty to write about. But I won't.

I'll just say that I shall always remember Koprivshtitsa because I left Little Pink there. I didn't leave him there because he was a bad horse or because Karo was better or because I didn't like him, because I thought a lot of Little Pink. I left him there because he was too young, that's all.

It was my fault. I'd bought too young a horse. I knew it when I bought him, but there hadn't been any choice. I'd gone round with Zhivko in his taxi and looked at every horse from Samokov to the moon. Little Pink and Karo had been the best ones.

On the trail in front of us were the Balkans. I just couldn't risk an excitable young horse fooling about on a cliff top. I'd have hated myself more to have lost him on a cliff top.

I sold him to the blacksmith.

I had a hard look at the man beforehand. He had a good house, two other horses both in fair order and a good stable. His son was a harness maker and showed me the harness they would use on Little Pink, and it was well made. But to think of him in harness again was hard. At least he would be a lot better off there than he had been in Samokov. There it was cool, he'd have a home he could call his own, and the winters were not severe. The town was a tourist place and the town horse copers took pride in how their horses were turned out. On top of this I sold him to a Bulgarian because I wouldn't have sold him to a gypsy.

In amongst all this, Chumpie left for England.

Zog came with Richard, his assistant, and they took Chumpie away. It was one of those wrenched partings where you don't say anything because there's somebody else there: you just part. Then about ten minutes later when you're back in your room you find a little note and then you wish they'd bring her back.

41

I tried to cheer myself up by spending most of the night with the horses, talking to them, grooming Little Pink and telling him what a good horse he was, but he knew I was leaving him. He knew I was going to go on alone with Karo and I know he knew by the way he was. Usually, when I groomed him, he fooled about trying to take the brush out of my hand. It was a game, we always played it: Little Pink was the funniest little horse. But that night he just stood still as if he was trying to work out what he'd done wrong, saying he wouldn't fool around anymore, if only I'd keep him.

And maybe this sounds like a pile of rot to those who keep stabled horses. But go and live with a horse night and day, spend all your time with him, ride him for eight hours a day every day, eat and sleep with him beside you, and you'll find out he has exactly the same moods and feelings as you do.

In the morning I saddled Karo and said goodbye to Little Pink and it broke my heart.

Karo

Karo had always been a shadowy figure for me up till then. I didn't really know him, at least not like I knew Little Pink. All I knew of him was what Chumpie told me about him and that he was always about a mile behind. I'd been so busy concentrating on Little Pink who'd see a tree trunk and look at it, then look at it, and he'd be looking at it so hard you'd think he'd stick to it, then his back legs would overtake the front ones like those Wait Disney animals, and all of a sudden he'd get bored of looking at that one and find another to look at until he'd nearly stuck to it and we'd have to do it all over again.

And Little Pink had this trick of belting off sideways every time something rattled around in a bush, so he was a bit of a jumpy ride in lots of ways, but that was only because he was a baby. Of course while all this was going on I didn't have much of a chance to see what Karo did. I found him much as Chumpie had described, which was slow. Karo was the slowest horse in the world. Every footstep took forever and sometimes he'd kind of put a foot out and wave it around like he was conducting the Philharmonic, then put it down and lurch forward, groaning. He did a lot of groaning, did Karo. Chumpie said he did. She said he grunted and wheezed and squeaked and groaned, and he did. He did all of those things. But he was a nice horse and very even tempered. Nothing fazed him: at least so it seemed, although he had one pet hate and I found out about that later when we went careering off down the road in front of a crane. Boy, did Karo hate cranes. The snag was, every time we fetched up on a tarmac road, which luckily wasn't that often, but every time we did every bloke in Bulgaria with a crane came creeping up behind us and I'd be in a daze, sort of half asleep, but Karo would see him and we'd go hammering off down the road in one big hurry, and that horse could shift when he wanted to. It was pretty frightening and actually now I'm scared of cranes too.

Anyway, the morning we left Koprivshtitsa I was feeling low. If there's one thing in the world I really hate, it's selling horses: I can't stand it. If I had my way I'd keep every horse I ever saw and have a huge great place full of them, but I suppose that's a bit of a dream.

Besides, I haven't got any money.

Anyway, off we went up this big hill the other side of Koprivshtitsa through a long pine plantation and out onto a huge high plateau and there was no one there. It was a lonely place. It made me feel even more lonely and exposed and it made Karo feel lonely too, I know it did. So there we were, alone on this huge high plateau with no one around us, just grass and wind, and it was a beautiful place, and I loved it although it made me lonely. About four or five miles further on we passed a big rambling old house in the middle of nowhere and there were dogs barking and one old horse tethered out on his own and he must have been much more lonely than Karo because he had to live there. A woman watched us as we went by. She was a gypsy, very dark, almost black. She didn't say anything. I didn't say anything. Just Karo and I went by in the wind and she watched us inching by.

It seemed to take a long time, that ride, and the reason it took a long time was because it did. That was when I fully realised how slow Karo was. It was unbelievable. He was buggered if he was going to go any quicker. I could try to whack him on with my legs but he didn't take the blindest bit of notice, so I thought of getting a twig and trying that, but we were in the most twigless place you've ever seen. Besides, he was all covered in saddlebags so it would have been impossible to do anything with a twig, so I just had to get used to creeping along, at his speed, which wasn't much.

Sometimes I wondered if we were actually moving at all. All the same, I liked him. I liked him because I've never seen a horse quite like Karo and I like funny-looking horses. He was a really old-fashioned looking horse, Karo. The kind of horse King Arthur probably sat on, with this big long body, pot-belly and short legs like they didn't really belong to him, and a big head with no brains in. That's not true actually: Karo was pretty smart. Any horse that gets his way the whole time is pretty smart. And someone up there loves Karo because he was the luckiest horse I ever knew.

Whenever we stopped somewhere, it was always just spot-on for Karo. He always wound up with the best grazing, was always the one who got tit-bits from the children, was always the one whom the old men patted, always the one who got the most comfortable bed, always the one who got the biggest dinner. Karo drew the long straw in life and you could tell it by his size. Karo weighed 650 kilograms, which is plenty for a 14.3 pony, and he weighed it all the way.

Valley of Roses

Karo and I fetched up in a place called Rosina, a town in central Bulgaria, where they grow about 140,000 acres of roses, for attar, rose oil. Apparently it takes three tons of petals to make one litre of oil, so it's pricey. They pick them early in the morning, at three or four, because after that the sun gets at them and the oil is not so good. The roses themselves are like dog roses, small and pink and grown on trellises, like vines. There's lavender there too and I rode through that with Karo. A black horse in 10,000 acres of lavender is a good sight and I got off him to take a photograph which was a bit of a mistake because I spent the rest of the day running around after him.

And I fluffed the photograph.

I stayed with a family who kept a small deer as a pet. They were a close-knit, warm family. The father was called Nikolai Nikol and he liked a drink. He also liked pork fat. So I got pork fat and raki, and that was supper, then we went to a restaurant, for more pork fat and raki. It was a great gloomy place, with these big flickering neon lights which give you a roaring headache. The restaurant was full of guys smashed out of their minds. There were gypsies in there too, but no one spoke to them because no one liked the gypsies. I remember their faces, torn, hunted, run-down faces, like brutalised wild animals.

Most of the people in this restaurant were drinking pretty rough raki at about fifteen pence a bottle and eating pork fat. What did they do with the pork itself? Throw it away? What was this with pork fat? I tell you, the diet in Eastern Europe was pretty rotten and even if everyone has a garden and grows his own vegetables and keeps his own animals, they've got a big thing going with pork fat and raki and if you want to feel really ill, go there.

It was in that town that I realised something else about Bulgarians and that is they are a people searching for a national identity. Ottoman occupation, followed by Russian domination and communist suppression, has left them not knowing who they really are. There are great ugly concrete monuments all over the place, portraying some local communist celebrity, but they don't feel right. You've got to dig pretty deep to get to know the real Bulgarian.

That night Nikolai took me off to a bar outside town where he sat down and jabbered away to a few of his mates, and I drank. Then this lovely girl just started singing, no accompaniment or anything. A friend of hers joined in and they sang a duet, every note in harmony, and I heard Bulgaria then. I heard the deepness of this girl's voice, how strong and rich it was, the plaintiveness of the song, the mood of the melody and the spell it cast on those drinkers.

It turned the night back six hundred years, and I heard the cry of Devils on Horseback, wind and snow in the Balkans, battles fought and won, I heard men calling and dying and saw dark rooms with carved beams and huge fires, fur coats and grizzled men with grizzled beards with blood-stained hands drinking from horns. I saw swords and pistols and something deep in the heart of all of them, half-grasped, slipping away, but remembered in that song.

There wasn't a dry eye in the place.

Nikolai, his wife and daughter led me away from the village down through the Valley of Roses and waved goodbye beneath an avenue of walnut trees. Karo and I walked into the rising sun past plough horses, old men scything, women bottoms up wielding hoes and carrying the hay scythed by the men. No one looked up. They were hard bitten, those people. Their lot was to work, face down, unquestioning, to stare into the earth all day and grow food because the promise of communism never materialised and for forty years it had failed to deliver.

On one side as we walked was Sredna Gora, the other Stara Planina, magnificent snow-dolloped mountains, and mountains Karo and I had to cross.

The Balkans

I didn't know where to cross; didn't have a map of the Balkans. So I reckoned to cross where things looked that way and when we got to Karlovo, we breezed into town and wandered off towards this vast mountain range and that's when Mustafa pitched up.

Mustafa is a Turk: an intellectual type. It was really strange to meet Mustafa. He addressed me in Turkish straight off, as though he knew I knew a bit of Turkish and so I said '*nasilsiniz arkadaş*' which means 'how's it going, my friend'. Then he spoke English and showed me the way to a path across the mountains. He introduced me to a some gypsies living at the bottom of the mountain and they were Turkish too. Most of the gypsies in Bulgaria are Turkish. They have two names, their own and a Bulgarian name. Todor Zhivkov decreed they should be called by their Bulgarian names. Of course, they don't like their Bulgarian names and don't use them on their own, only in public. And there'd been bad blood lately too, violence and killings. Some Turks – gypsies – decided they'd had enough of this and went back to Turkey. On arrival they found there was no work, nothing for them, so they were forced to return, and this weakened their already weak position. It wasn't good. They have a tough time of it, the Turks, the gypsies in Bulgaria.

'*Mashallah*!' they said when they saw Karo. '*At çok guzel!*'

Then one of them kissed him across the top of his head, put his hand on his head and said '*mashallah!*' again. It invokes the blessing of Allah: I know that, I remember it from my Turkish ride.

I really like the Turks.

So old Mustafa waffled on about Turkey and the elections, gave me details of an address in Istanbul, which was kind of him, but it was a bit of a ride from where we were just then, and then he pointed up the mountain.

'Is that it?' I asked.

He nodded. Meaning yes.

'What, that rock? That's a path?'

He nodded again. I gave it another look. It didn't look much like a path. More like a temporarily-stopped avalanche. Mustafa looked at me, then at the path and said 'Follow it'. On the principle that everything in life always turns up at the right time (usually just the nick of time), up we went – and wasn't that a prize brute to climb!

I was leading Karo, not riding of course, and halfway up I began to think Mustafa was in league with the commies and was trying to do away with Karo and me, puffing our hearts out. Then Karo wedged both front feet in a tiny gap in a rock and panicked because he couldn't get them out and that was the first shoe off. That path went on and on, rising higher and higher and at one time we seemed to be right on the very edge trying to get up the next bit and I thought we'd never get back down because old Karo was thrashing around on these rocks and he was pretty scared. So was I. He was sweating too. So was I.

I'm not good at heights and I tell you, the Balkans are high.

That's where I remembered Zog.

'The Balkans kill.'

It was just about midday then, and cloud was beginning to drift around. You could hear all this booming and thundering going on. Big mountains often seem to boom and thunder. I don't know what it is.

And Karo kept on looking down so you could see the whites of his eyes and he watched these little stones as they rolled and bounced away, so I tried to stop him looking down and up we went again. Then we had to go down into a gorge and that was pure hell. But there was a river in that gorge and it had worn the rocks away smooth as knucklebones. They were big though, and

white, and the river raced through them, clear water, white water, and that water tasted good. Karo must have drunk half the river before we set off again but we didn't have to cope with any more vertical ascents. It turned into one big walk through trees and woodland and all the way we followed these little signs to Hija Levski.

Now a hija is a funny thing. It isn't a hotel but it is a hotel. In Bulgaria you can be standing right next to a hija and ask some old duck or other if there's a hotel anywhere and she'll say no. Then you try changing your tack and ask if there's a kon-dom and a place for you to stay and she'll say no again. So then you ask if there's anything else remotely like a hotel with a kon-dom and she'll still say no. But if you ask if there's a hija, she'll say yes, you're standing right next to it. And a hija is exactly like a hotel in that it has beds, and you can eat maybe, and even get a drink, and sometimes they have bars and swimming pools and all the kinds of things hotels have, but they're not hotels, they're hijas. I knew somewhere where we were headed there was supposed to be a hija called Hija Levski, and I can tell you it's a frigging long walk from Karlovo. Especially if you're hanging on to a fat pony who's scared of heights and even more of a long walk if you're scared of heights too.

Anyway, we got there. Whacked. It's right in the middle of nowhere, a big building with 3-phase electricity running off a water turbine. There was a radio-telephone and that was it. It felt very out of the way. The fellow running it was called Genko Genkov and he was a mountain man. Genko had a beard and those cool clear eyes people who live in mountains have from looking far off all the time. He knew the routes across. He told me to stay for one night and then in the morning he'd show me the way for Ambaritsa, another hija. It meant Karo having to spend the night outside on his own and there are bears up there, plenty. Bears like horses. To eat, that is. So I wrapped him up in blankets to keep him warm because it was cold there, gave him barley which Genko had and stayed with him until I was too pooped to stay any longer and went to bed half hanging out of the window upstairs so I could keep an eye on him.

As good as his word Genko led us the next day away from Hija Levski out on a tiny path that ran north towards Ambaritsa. When we came out of the forest I saw the real size of the Balkans. They are *big* mountains. They plunge down into huge gorges, and sweep right up into the cloud so you can't see the tops. We were in a vast amphitheatre, craggy and windblown, cold and misty, and we followed this little path zigzagging across the scree, and then Genko took a right turn and we went straight up.

There was a lake up there. A little one – frozen solid – and this was May. Great slabs of snow hung in deep sweeping arcs and when we came to a saddle in the rock, Genko pointed off down and north and told me Ambaritsa was down there. I thought he said go on for six hundred metres then go right and you'll see it. We were in cloud and I couldn't see a thing.

'The cloud will go soon,' he said, turned round and beat it.

I was pretty unsure about all this. I don't like being in fog in mountains and Karo was very edgy. A few times the ground had slipped beneath his weight and he'd lost his footing. Added to this his remaining three shoes were polished and he was sliding badly. But I didn't hang about up there wondering what to do, but got straight on with it and led Karo for what I counted out to be six hundred metres, then turned right and it was still foggy.

The hill dropped away sharply, one long grass slope. I could see maybe a thousand feet or so down and it was straight down. There was a tiny little sheep path there, but it was steep. As I was looking at it, the cloud shifted and I caught a glimpse of a white building way below us, about two thousand feet. Ambaritsa. I caught hold of the reins tightly, told Karo not to rush it, which he was inclined to do when scared, and we set off gingerly along that path. Around us was an empty brooding world.

'The Balkans kill.'

There was nothing there but us and the mountains and the wind. Genko would never have heard me if I called. He'd gone.

And I don't know quite what happened, but we were on that path one minute, with these little rocks rolling off down the mountainside, when I realised the ground was not holding Karo's weight. He pulled back on his hocks to stop himself and then we both went.

The shock whipped my breath away.

It seemed to go on and on and the world was roaring past; one minute I was looking up at the sky, the next down into the valley with grass thrashing into my eyes like needles and Karo facing this way then that. At one time he seemed to be sitting on his backside with his front legs stretched out, ears pricked, then he was on his side and the saddle and all had slipped up and was pulling, then he was fighting for footing like Bambi on ice and when all of a sudden we came thumping to a halt, I round a juniper bush and Karo on a sheep trail. I reckon I'm the only bloke who's tobogganed down the Balkans in spring with a horse and without a toboggan.

I was so shaky I couldn't get up.

Neither could Karo.

He was heaving and panting and gulping and chomping at his bit, and I was certain he must have broken his legs and what was I going to do then?

I got to my feet all of a wobble at the same time as Karo got to his all of a wobble and we stood there in front of one another wobbling.

I don't know how long we stood staring at one another wobbling but the big snag was we'd covered about a thousand feet in what felt like about three seconds and there were still another thousand to go.

We got down after a very frightening descent, because old Karo only wanted to go up, though heaven knows why, and he kept on trying to graze, which didn't help, and when we got to this confounded place we found it was not Ambaritsa at all but a shepherd's hut, and abandoned.

I yelled. And yelled and yelled and yelled.

I was lost and those words came back: 'The Balkans kill.'

About four hours later, exhausted, we found Ambaritsa, and were welcomed by a man with all the charm of a recent deposit of catshit.

'*Nyama bira*, he said. No beer.

'*Nyama voda*,' he said. No water.

'*Nyama sitchko*.' No nothing. Then he pushed off, leaving Karo and me desolate.

But Karo's a lucky horse and it didn't take long for me to find him a patch of clover Karo-size and so he ate. I slept in intermittent sunshine.

That night we were off the Balkans and that was a long walk from Ambaritsa. I groomed Karo as the sun went down, and noticed he'd lost weight. But I noticed something else too: we were closer. We were closer because we'd shared an intense experience and he looked at me as if to say, 'Well, we did it, didn't we?' and he brought a tear to my eye. He had one shoe left and his hocks were bruised, he had cuts on his flanks and the hair on his right side was all shorn off and burned from the fall. The saddle bags were ripped and the stitching bust. I had a broken finger and a broken toe.

That was the roughest crossing I've ever made.

Thanks, Zog, for the warning. I believe the Balkans kill: yes, I believe it.

But they didn't kill us.

Karo's a brave horse, Zog, no kidding.

Runaway

I had Karo re-shod in Oreshak, the shoeing made spectacular only by its eccentricity. But they were better than nothing and we slogged on to Troyan monastery.

These Bulgarian monasteries are funny places because they're not hijas, not hotels, they're monasteries, but you can stay in them, and they're cheap. One night for Karo and me was two quid. You don't get much to eat for that but in Troyan there's a restaurant, and that's where I was sitting when a dyed-by-her-own-hand blonde lady of many sultry summers, came to sit down beside me and asked me if I wanted to slip off with her in her car before her old man turned up. She took a bit of shaking off because she reckoned I was carrying dollars, which was right, and she was keen on those.

Just about everybody in Bulgaria is keen on dollars because their economy is up the creek and most of the time their money isn't worth a lot. There are touts all over the place and every single person I met showed more than a passing interest in having a good look at a dollar, or ten, or a hundred and then asked if they could have them. They seemed to think I was some kind of roving millionaire, and when I told them I lived in a crumbling shack on a hillside with no electricity and it takes me forever to make ten quid, they didn't believe it.

And the thing about monasteries is they close at night. I know. I had to climb in over the roof.

Despite that, Troyan is pretty nice actually. I got a good view of it; even though it was dark at the time. It's got these big galleried quadrangles with the cells off them, which are the hotel rooms, and there's a little church with painted frescoes and inside it just sparkles with gold and pungent with incense. There's another acid old woman in there who won't let you take any snaps and she was pretty sour. But otherwise it's fine, Troyan, even if you do have to climb in over the roof. And it's very good after champagne at fifty pence a bottle, which is good stuff for climbing about on roofs.

All the characters I was drinking it with thought Karo was a pretty good horse too.

'*Hubavo koni!*' they all bawled. 'What a good horse!'

He was. He was a heck of a good horse, Karo.

Anyway next day I had a blazing headache and shuffled off to a place called Stolit, stayed there for the night and that's when Karo vanished.

I'd tethered him in a stand of grass on a long line. I kept an eye on him, of course, but had to slip off to the town to buy a few things for myself because I was half starved and my clothes were in bits. When I came back he'd gone.

First of all I thought he'd been stolen because there were a lot of gypsies round there, so what I did was go straight to them and ask.

No, they hadn't seen a runaway horse but Vesco Asenov Filev, a gypsy, said, 'The way to catch a horse is with another one!', and produced two ponies. Off we went bareback and the hunt was on.

He could ride, Vesco, and we went belting off here, there and everywhere looking for Karo. We went to the big gypsy place outside Stolit and asked there, but no one had seen him.

'They won't have taken him,' Vesco said. '*Tsigani* do not steal.' And something about his words made me think he was right. Half an hour later there was a great crash, a squeal, a thundering of hooves and out of a pile of bushes burst Karo yelling his head off.

I don't know where he'd been, but he looked pretty pleased to be back, and Vesco took him to his place and kept him there for the night. And didn't he feed him! That was when I regretted thinking I'd never seen a gypsy handle a horse well, because Vesco could and he was prefect with them.

I liked Vesco's old man too. He was called Assen. He was a real old soak, but he was funny. That night I had a meal with Vesco and his old man Assen sitting under a swinging single bulb on the verandah of his bit-of-a-shambles house, by the river. The horses were stuffing themselves on lucerne and Vesco was pouring out raki when a car drew up and out got the local communist fat-cat, out to swing a few votes.

Now Vesco's old man Assen had just been waffling on about what a crowd of crooks the commies were and this heavyweight sat down trying to sweet-talk him into voting for him in the elections, but he just sat there doodling his foot in the dirt and puffing away on his fag. Then the commie chief said he'd left his fags in the car and could he have one of Assen's, which he took, with a bit of raki, and a quarter of an hour later he cleared off.

'Old Assen wasn't unhappy to see him go and bitched on for a few minutes about what kind of a stinker he thought he was, then suddenly old Assen jumps up and starts patting his pockets.

'The stinker!' he shouts as the car drives away, and he searches the ground, pats his pockets again, looks under the table, and then bursts out laughing.

'The stinker!' he shouted again and took a big drink and then Vesco was laughing and everyone was laughing except me; then I got it.

The stinker had walked off with his fags.

Before I left next morning Assen poured me a big tumbler of raki.

'*Sherife!*' he said. It's Turkish: a toast.

I like the Turks, and I don't care if they're gypsies or whatever they are, I like them.

From there on the weather got hotter. I was heading in the direction of Ruse hoping to exit to Romania but what was eating me up was the whole business of exporting Karo. I didn't want to have to sell him at the frontier because he was a good horse and he was my friend, and I hate selling horses, as I've mentioned before. But everything I had was wrong. I didn't have any proper papers saying how he was bred, because he was a pure-bred horse: there was this great brand, 316, on him which said so, which made me certain he was a pinched horse and so maybe I was accessory to the crime, or whatever it's called. And even if the scrap of paper did count for anything, I'd bought him for leva at the reduced tourist rate rather than at the bank rate and so all things were stacking up to a load of hitches.

But what can you do?

I thought of going to Gabrovo, which is supposed to be a city where they tell a lot of jokes all day, to see what kind of a joke they could make out of that, but since I hadn't got that much of a handle on the language I didn't think it was worth my while. After a few days' slogging we arrived up in Velika Turnovo. We'd just been through a lot of Cotswold-like scenery and it had been hot. We spent the night in a closed campsite where I left Karo filling his portly form with grass while I went to visit the town. I met four English women and they were great to be with because they had a thirst for champagne at fifty pence a bottle, although I seem to remember it cost more than that but we drank it anyway. Then they disappeared and I wandered round town feeling dizzy. I missed them. They were all really bright and full of knowledge and to be with them was like fresh air. I was sorry they had to go.

It's picturesque, Velika Turnovo. The river winds along in a deep valley through the middle of town. There's a big rambling old fortress on the hill opposite where they have a *son-et-lumiere*.

The town houses are wood-frame construction, tiered outward on the top where vines have been trained, so the effect is very foreign to English eyes. Some houses have stucco-work and painted brickwork and the doors are mostly natural wood coloured. The outskirts of the place are concrete, as ever, and ruined.

The first round of elections were on while I was there, and everyone was excited. The radio said there were 150,000 CDC – that's democratic votes – to 100,000 communist, or BCP as they styled themselves.

The commies won needless to say, despite there being official observers from other countries. I don't know how but I wound up in the company of a born-again Christian and she and two others were the only ones who voted to get King Simeon back. And there was a young fellow who was so disappointed the communists won he burst into tears. There were demonstrations. The people in town didn't like the communists winning. They sat in the road and chanted 'Rig! Rig!' They sang patriotic songs and waved blue flags, the colour of CDC. I asked if this all meant a new beginning.

'No. But it's the beginning of the end.'

Then somebody said 'No: it's the end of the beginning.'

Well I didn't know what it was, so went back and got Karo and we pushed off.

We spent another night in another monastery impossibly called Preobrazenski Manactir where an old French-speaking monk told me the birds were trying to say something because they were flocking and they never flocked at that time of year. He wore a purple three-cornered hat and was pretty interested in a pair of new jeans I'd bought and asked if they might fit him. He was a very nice old man, that monk. There was something very special about him. He was a very gentle old man and when he spoke you listened. I shared a meal with him, just lentils, he being vegetarian. I watched him as he ate and talked, and recognised there was something intensely delicate and sensitive about him, something really very fine, kind and gentle.

There was a wild gypsy staying there at the same time too. He was called Xristo. He was very inquisitive, Xristo. He was a bit different from the old monk.

Did I have a wife? No? Then did I want one, a Bulgarian one? I ought to go and look at Vasili's wife: she was a good one: a big fat one with big tits and she was a bit of all right. He wouldn't mind one like Vasili's got. What colour hair did I like them with? He liked the ones with blonde hair and no pubes. That's what he liked best. He'd seen one like that in a magazine. Were there any like that in England? Could I fix him up with one? How much? She had to be unspoiled, mind: he wouldn't want any old one, especially after some filthy Englishman had been prodding about with her, no, not him, he didn't want a used one. And what about my boots? Where did they come from? How much? How much was the horse? Did I want another? What about a drink? Can I play poker? Did I want a woman? He did. Maybe he'd slip off and see if Vasili was out. Silly old bugger that old monk, isn't he? Now what about this drink.

Actually, he was pretty exhausting, Xristo.

Cut-throat

Karo and I slipped away just before sunrise from Preobrazenski Manactir and wound our way down through the woodland as dawn was lighting the tops of the trees.

There are big gulleys all round Velika Turnovo and they're difficult to cross on horseback, so we had to get on to the road, and the very first thing along that road was a crane, so we left Velika Turnovo faster than I'd planned.

I was hoarse for the rest of the day after that, even though the weather was hot, too hot to ride, so we spent most of the day holed up in shade.

There was a fellow there with a tractor going round and round this field rowing up a nice crop of fathen. Every time he went past he waved. He must have waved a thousand times. When he'd rowed up most of the fathen he came across to Karo and me. He was a bit like Xristo.

How old was I?
How much did the horse cost?
Would I sell the saddle?
Would I sell the horse?
How many dollars have I got?
Has my wife got blonde hair?
What? No wife? Am I going to get a Bulgarian one?
Where am I going to sleep?
How many days have I been in Bulgaria?
Would I like to see his horse?

Everybody seemed to be full of questions, so I asked a few:

Which is the quickest way to Romania?
How far is it?
Why doesn't he get back on his tractor and plough up a bit more fathen?

Above: The blue-denimed
man in Kovachevski

Right: Dancing bear

Left: Zhivko and Mitko

Below: Little Pink and Karo delivered

Opposite: Chumpie with Karo

Above: He was a nice bald old man

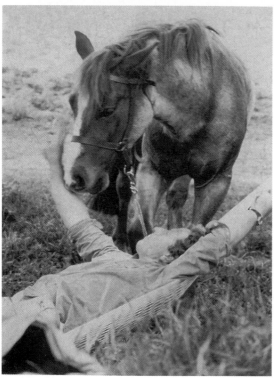

Left: Little Pink was an affectionate horse

A grazing break en route. Chumpie stitching some running repairs

The honeycomb man

Above right: If only you could see...
Above left: Flehman
Below: André

Above: Sandu, Tudor and Gheorghe Martinescu

Left: André and Puşa

Above: The Carpathians are beautiful

Left: André and the horses outside Çeauçescu's shooting lodge

Anyway, he just squatted there on his haunches peering into my saddlebags for a bit, then got back on his tractor and ploughed a bit more fathen and Karo and I left sometime when the sun was lower.

We wound up boiled in Dve Mogili a few days later, round about midday. We were both really thirsty and it was hot. There's a square in the middle of Dve Mogili with a statue of some brute brandishing a pair of revolvers and near him is a conked-out fountain. Karo knows how to drink out of fountains and sucks on them, like teats, and I've never seen anybody look as miserable as he did when we got to that fountain and found it conked out.

There were all these people sitting on park benches in the shade of trees in the square, so I went up to them and asked them for water and they all nodded, meaning no, they didn't know where we could get water.

I don't like my horse going thirsty and don't much like it myself, no one was going to help us, and just then I didn't think much of Bulgarians. For one hour we walked round that place and though I asked and asked no one gave us water.

Then a little fellow, a *tsigani*, a gypsy, a dirty, stubbly little fellow came up to me and took me by the arm and led me to a side street and went into a house and brought out water. Karo drank three buckets straight off.

Then I took that little guy back out into the square and we tethered Karo under the trees and I went into a restaurant and asked for beer.

'*Nyama*,' they said. No beer. I know my eyes flashed. I was angry.

I pulled out dollars and said I'd pay double and took back to Mihmoon, the little guy under the trees, the little gypsy who gave me water, I took him a case of beer.

Then all his friends came, gypsies all of them: lovely dark-eyed giggling girls, their gold-toothed mothers, fat and greasy, their boss-eyed boyfriends, stubbly and warty, and other friends, filthy fingered and dressed in rags and I bought another case of beer and there, right in front of all those Bulgarians, I entertained the town's gypsies slap bang in the town square because it was a gypsy who'd given me water.

'Amare shokar Develevski!' they bawled, the gypsy toast.
'Nasdravye!' I toasted back.
'Sherife!' someone shouted.
'Cheers!' I countered.
'Amare shokar Develevski!'

The park attendant came along to throw us off, but he got booed. Then the police came and everybody scattered and Mihmoon took me to another place to finish off the beer and I bought another case. Karo was housed in some black old stable, given pea haulms and barley and I went out on the town with Mihmoon and we were pretty plastered.

Now the thing I liked about that lot was they were alive.

I'd been staying in villages where they kept their chickens and pigs, where there was never anywhere to wash, where the food was always pork fat and raki, where the people were always tight fisted and conservative and didn't want to change. They wanted things to stay like they were. They were a real 'I'm all right Jack' community and though they put me and my horse up, I thought them narrow. They were an unsmiling people.

Their houses were always the same, they all had radios outside the back door, they all had three pigs and ten chickens and ten geese and all these vegetables and lived tight little lives working in the collective and if anybody did anything to rock the boat they got it in the neck from the *kmet*. I remember one guy, a big burly, bully of a man listening to the radio one morning and when he heard that CDC were polling better than BCP in Sofia, he stabbed the kitchen table with a fork.

So when I was plastered with Mihmoon and falling about the place, saying all the commies were crooks and slobbering beer over ourselves, with all these other gypsies whooping and wolf whistling and smacking each other about, I had a thought and this was it:

A gypsy sold me my horse, and a gypsy helped me find him when he ran off. It was a gypsy who showed me the way back in Karlovo and a gypsy who gave me water. It was the gypsies who made me laugh and the gypsies who brought life back into a trip which was flagging. And the night went on and we went to this place and this place and this place and drank beer and raki and some filthy green wine, and we laughed and joked and most of the time I was in fits because Mihmoon was very funny, and what with these other crazy characters all smashed out of their minds showing the tourist the gypsy hot spots, it turned into quite a night and I thought a lot of them.

But, on a park bench way past midnight, Mihmoon pulled a knife on me and robbed me of a couple of hundred dollars.

I felt such a fool.

I watched him run off, stagger off, through the trees and I was sweating. Probably it was the beer and the fright of a smiling face suddenly turned ugly and my own weakness in failing to overpower him, but the shock was immense. I couldn't say if he'd have driven that knife into me, but he looked bitter and twisted enough to do it.

I dossed down in a pit full of mothballs that night and felt like I'd been exhumed in the morning. It was pelting when I cleared town with my let-the-wet-in poncho and a hangover and felt a real class-act idiot. I wondered if there was a special Town-Clown medal awarded to people like me in Dve Mogili. I tried to throttle myself.

Just outside town I saw a figure slopping along the road toward me. A little fellow, hunched up in the rain, with his jacket over his head. He was right in the middle of the road and the road was grey from the rain.

It was Mihmoon.

I knew he'd seen me: couldn't have missed me sitting up there on Karo.

I thought to run the man down.

But he didn't get off the road and just carried on walking toward me. I rode right up to him and he looked up.

His eyes were like a pair of old poached eggs, all brown and murky. He stopped and looked up and the rain was running off his chin. He pulled his hands out of his pockets and the linings of his pockets as well, and he pulled a face. He was skint.

No, he wasn't skint: he'd been robbed.

It took me a second or two: then I burst out laughing. So did he. I laughed louder. So did he. I don't know why I laughed but maybe it was because we were the same: we'd both been robbed, both were wet, both felt ill, and both had no home: maybe that was it.

Then I bent down and shook his hand and he wished me '*Pryatin put!*' – 'Safe road!' We were in stitches. He waved me goodbye, telling me to come back one day, wishing me good luck and Godspeed, and I saw him stand there in the pouring rain, waving away.

I liked Mammon.

He gave me water.

Across the Danube

The bloke who shod Karo outside Dve Mogili wasn't what you would call a top-notch farrier. Karo would have been better shod by Mihmoon after a couple of bottles of raki and Mihmoon was scared stiff of horses. This bloke cut Karo's toes off. He hardly had any nails either. Still, he was better than a bloke in Romania some time later who turned up with a hammer and a bicycle pump and God knows what he planned to do but I wouldn't let him.

Old Karo coped though, and the road to Ruse wasn't long – except nobody had any food along it, nothing was open, you couldn't buy a drink, there was no water and everybody seemed to drag themselves about as though nearly dead.

On top of this, although I was keen to get out of Bulgaria because I'd been there six weeks and wanted to see Romania, everyone was putting the wind up me saying what a shocking place it was, full of crooks and thieves, that it was far too dangerous to go on a horse and that I'd be lucky to get out alive. Everyone said it. And they said there was no grub, the water stank, everybody had AIDS, there wasn't any beer – nothing: nothing at all. It was one big dump.

'They are bad neighbours,' one authority advised me.

It gets to you, stuff like that. I was a bit windy to tell you the truth.

Then there was the business of language because I didn't know one word of Romanian and was just getting the hang of Bulgarian and having to cope with new money, new words, and people who kill you and steal all your kit was heavy.

And of course I had to do all Karo's papers. I wanted to keep Karo '*Hubavo kon!*' everyone said, and patted him.

I'll always remember the family who put Karo and me up in Ruse. I'll remember them because Nikolai Kolev and his father-in-law Ivan Ivanov had a four-bottle-a-day thirst for malt whisky, provided by me, from the dollar shop. I tried telling Ivan Ivanov that whisky and sun was a bad combination. I tried. When he started mixing copper sulphate up in a pair of tights thrown into a saucepan I knew it was time for him to drink the rest of the bottle.

'Nasdravye!' he gargled, smashing his glass into Nikolai's. (They're strong, Bulgarian glasses. They have to be.)

'Nasdravye!' Nikolai roared back. Smash! Clang! Glug, glug, glug. Golden liquid oozed over the table, over hands, aimed vaguely into unsteady glasses.

'Nasdravye Chirimee!' Clang! Smash!

'Aha! Bulgariski raboti!'

'CDC!'

'Nasdravye CDC!'

After they'd seen the best part of four malts off, Ivan Ivanov garbled something about BCP in Velika Britania (England). Was it a problem? And didn't we have a Tsarina or someone? Or women doing all the politics or something? And there he was swaying about slobbering away on a bar of Toblerone and his fag and this whisky; he was a bit of a soak too, old Ivan Ivanov, and deaf; deaf as a post he was.

And Nikolai must have reckoned I was the Wandering Jew or something because he just couldn't get it into his head my dollars were limited, and wanted to go to the dollar shop the whole time.

'Chirimee,' he said. *'Dollarrr? Schiop?'* And off we'd go. God, I'm a mug.

But they had nothing, those people. Nikolai and Christina lived in a concrete monstrosity in Ruse with nothing. They heated their water by tossing an electric filament into it with its wires hanging out. It was a killer, but didn't fuse because the wiring in those flats didn't have fuses.

'Bulgariski raboti!' Christina wailed. Bulgarian work!

They were rough, those flats, and there's a sea of them outside Ruse. The centre of Ruse wasn't bad though. It was mostly rococo, some of the buildings pretty, with lots of style. The centre was big and airy.

The second round of the elections was going on too and people were gathering on street corners waving flags and yelling, but mostly everyone looked bored. I mean, how exciting is an election? You get some politico shouting his mouth off, and another shouting his mouth off, and actually you wouldn't give the steam off a gallon of hot horse piss for the lot of them.

Nikolai put on a show of being interested for about three seconds before asking about another visit to the dollar shop and that time he wound up with a cassette recorder. If I hear 'left bum and ipsitum left by yooouuu' or whatever that song is ever again I'll kill myself.

I was washing my hair in the shower in Nikolai's flat when the water and the electricity went off both at the same time. No one was in the least surprised. They shrugged their shoulders.

'*Bulgariski raboti!*'

'*Nyama voda!*'

'*Nyama* current!'

... left bum and ipsitum left by yooouuuu ...

You can see Romania from Ruse. It's just across the Danube. All you see is a line of trees and a spout gulching muck into the river. There's a walloping big factory as well. Everyone complains.

I was looking at it from the patio of some snazzy hotel where all these kids were dolled up and drinking orange squash. Those clothes looked expensive. Western kit.

'Where do they get those clothes Nikolai?'

'Black market.'

'Where do they get the dollars?'

'Black market.'

'How?'

'*Tsigani.*'

It looks like the whole country would collapse without the *tsigani* because they keep the black market running. What a place.

A German fellow pitched up with a couple of others off a ferry . They were on a cruise. They'd been to Yalta. He was a distinguished sort of a bloke with a hooked nose and important looking eyebrows. He talked about Eastern Germany. He didn't hold out much hope for them.

'Ten years,' he said. 'They'll be in a mess for ten years.' I remembered that when I got there.

The election results were announced on my last night in Ruse. The commies got back in. BCP.

'Well?' I asked.

Nikolai shrugged his shoulders. 'Even if CDC got in, the ones who'd be running the country would be the same as now. Politicians.'

Then we went to the dollar shop again: one last spree. He's an expensive kind of a mate, Nikolai.

I voiced my doubts about getting across the border, and even though the vet had seen Karo and a so-called Coggins test had been done, I couldn't see it working.

'*Nyama problem!*' Nikolai roared, and fetched out one of the new bottles. As the metal stopper cracked in his hands, he winked.

'*Nyama problem! Mitnitsa nyama problem!*'

A few days later with his help, a vet, two bottles of malt whisky, a few cartons of cigarettes, and Nikolai's mate who worked inside the customs – the nyama problem man – a handful of dollars, a Coggins test and a gutful of oats for Karo, I stood on the bridge over the Danube waving goodbye to Nikolai, Christina and his family, goodbye to Bulgaria.

I was sorry to leave.

Reflections

It's long, the bridge over the Danube. There's a train that runs underneath it so the whole thing shakes like meccano and there you are trying to hang on to your pony with this terrific din going on under his feet and the whole world wobbling about, and I tell you, don't cross the Danube with a horse.

On the far side of the bridge – if you make it, if you and your horse haven't gone piling over the edge because of the train – is the pride of the Romanian army on sentry duty picking its nose. You can tell the difference the minute you hit land on the far side. And that's when you start thinking about everything everyone said about being killed and beaten up and robbed and fleed and the horse '*heidiiii!!!*' I thought back, just then.

Rural Bulgaria is magnificent. The old monasteries and the Balkans spectacular. Chumpie and I witnessed the dying throes of communism, how those who had known how to exploit it for their own benefit were determined to hang on at any cost. The last thing they wanted was change. The last thing most *people* wanted was change. Built into the national psyche is fear of a new, unknown oppressor. This, somehow, it seemed to me, caused them all to share the same kind of mind: they laughed at the same jokes, said the same things, from one part of the country to the other.

It was stagnant. And stagnancy had led to complacency. Complacency being the only attitude you can have under an oppressive regime when the brightest, honest sparks live the shortest lives. Stagnancy promotes cunning, it promotes corruption, it brings to power the worst kind of people in any society. In places like this, power always falls to the ones who lack any moral compass. If you want to survive, you keep your head down; look into the dirt all day, say nothing, repeat the same safe stories, hide behind the same safe walls, ask for nothing, seek nothing – and exist. The country itself was lovely. You don't see country like that in Western Europe. Not with huge great fields and no fences. I reckon

I rode about seven or eight hundred kilometres through Bulgaria and never saw a fence. That's good riding country. In total I reckon we did about fifty kilometres only on tarmac. And there are thousands of acres of forestry, big broadleaf woodlands, a real treasure. And the Balkans were truly impressive. I didn't like them at the time because they tried to kill us, but looking back, you want to go there. Walk them. You'll be happy if you walk them. There's not a soul up there, except Genko Genkov, and if he says he'll show you the way to Ambaritsa, make the blighter take you there, never mind the fog.

There was one day I remember. It was one of those days when the air was so hard and clear you felt if you flicked it, it'd ring. Karo and I were going along past this collective, and switched down through a bit of a valley, then came up in a huge field of wheat. Must have been a three thousand acre field.

There was this little dirt track running right the way down it and so we followed it and on either side the corn was just turning so it was kind of greeny-gold and feathery. Right in the distance was a huge smoky blue wood and a line of purple low hills. Then just about halfway along this little road were tracks, animal tracks running off through the crop. Now we never trample crop but there were tracks and I thought a couple of cowboys must have ridden that way.

I hadn't seen another mounted horseman so Karo and I followed those tracks. They weaved all over the place. Two horses I reckoned, not big, but two. And the jockeys must have been drunk, they were all over the place. We went on following them up a hill, and just as we hit the other side there were the biggest pair of stags you've ever seen. Those antlers must have stuck up four feet, and stuck out six. They were beauties. And they didn't care much about us, but just looked at us with their black eyes and then slowly loped away with their white tails and big hindquarters going, and that was the finest sight I've seen in years.

Stallion Man

So there we were standing at the customs, and a bus driver sidles over and says, 'You can't go into Romania with a horse, he'll be stolen. Maybe you'll be killed.'

Then he stubs his fag out and shakes his head and then another leans out of his truck and shakes his head and says, 'You'll never make it,' and wags his finger, like you're a real berk even thinking of it.

The customs bloke took one look at my papers.

On a horse? Do you know how big Romania is? Where are you going? What!!! OK, here's your transit visa. Yes, yes, you're in.

Just the other side of the customs point is a camping place. I don't know how many frothing mugs of fly-filled beer I was offered or how many hands patted Karo, or how many gypsy faces I looked into, with rows of platinum teeth. I just don't know. Talk about friendly.

'Of course you can ride through Romania! The *tsigani* will help you! This is *tsigani* country! Course you won't be robbed! Have you got any dollars? The Romanian for a horse is '*cai*'. Romanian is Latin. The Romanian for farmer is '*agricola*'. Meet my wife: she's called Olympia. No, no: we're not called Romanian, we're Roman. You know, Rome: Roman. Yes, it's like Italian only with a few funny things thrown in to mess you about a bit. Yes is '*da*'. That's it: like Russian. '*Priaten*' is friend, like Bulgarian. The money is called *lei*. No, don't go and change it in the bank, they only give you twenty to the dollar. Change it with the *tsigani*, they'll give you a much better deal, hundred to the dollar – more maybe.

'Yes, the miners beat up the students. Yes, Illeascu is a crook. All commies are crooks. Didn't you know? But he's not as big a crook as Çeauçescu. I could tell you a few things about him.

'Do you know about the bears? I'll tell you about the bears. Çeauçescu had shooting lodges shoved up all over the place, then used to come along with a bunch of his cronies and lean out of the balcony and blaze away at bears. It was easy for them to do this because the villagers were forced to stake goats out to make the bears come down from the mountains. So every week they staked out a goat or two and down came the bears. When they shot Çeauçescu, nobody told the bears. But the bears kept coming. There weren't any goats so they ate the villagers' children instead. Didn't you know this story?'

I stayed with a gypsy that night. I'll describe his place because I haven't given you much of an idea about how these gypsies live.

His place was round the back of Giurgiu down a dirt street. It had big old wooden gates to it and in the garden, which was about a hundred feet by a hundred, there were plum trees, and a washing line, and a well. There's no piped water in any of the villages in Romania so everyone has a well. The wells are all hand bored and they're deep.

This fellow was a settled gypsy, like most of them, and kept animals and his place was a real pit. There was shit everywhere. Mostly chickens' and pigs', and the pigs were kept in a horrific hole beside the stable which was a crumbling ruin where his stallion lived.

In the yard were a couple of wrecked carts and a heap of rotting dung and the whole place was smothered in flies. The house was low, like a little bungalow and it stank of pee. It was gaily decorated though, with tapestries in very bright colours, and they suited the hot climate. He had furniture, mass-produced stuff, a big ugly cabinet with a glass front, with deodorants and shampoos, and empty bottles of whisky inside – they put western goods on display.

He had a pretty wife, and she was big, and these two big-eyed dark brown babies and they were a knockout.

He worked with his horse, delivering goods, and mostly he was pretty poor. He worked his stallion till that horse frothed at the mouth from exhaustion. I can't stand to see it.

Of course this fellow took a bit of a shine to Karo and he wanted to have him, because alongside his stallion Karo looked really great. He was all of a gloss, and he was confident: Karo's got a lot of presence anyway. In that twilight, he rippled muscle, but then Karo's a strong horse.

Anyway, I was grooming Karo when this guy pushed off for a bit, then came back and took that stallion out of harness and turned him into that filthy shed without food or water like he was the laziest creature on earth, and that horse was hungry and tired and just about on his last legs. So what I did was this.

I tried to get across to this fellow that he had a good horse, but he replied that his horse was stupid and so I said I didn't think his horse looked stupid and I'd show him something to prove it. I told him his horse was just as good as Karo and he was a fine looking horse but he needed a bit of attention. So I got him out of his stable, and he was a pretty angry horse because he thought he was going to have to do more work. Anyway, he simmered down, and I washed him. I cut his tail and groomed him and polished him up and made that gypsy give him water. I don't know why people won't give horses water. I tell you, the world is full of dehydrated horses. Where does this idiotic idea come from? I made him give that horse a lot of water and told him he'd be as big as Karo if only he gave him water. And I made him give him food: lucerne. That horse ate that lucerne like he'd never eaten in his whole life, and maybe he hadn't. Then I poured some wormer down the poor beggar because I always carry wormer and reckoned his need was greater than Karo's. It must have been midnight when that horse dried off, and had eaten himself to a standstill and he looked really different. You know, that horse had four white socks? You wouldn't have believed it. So by the light of a solitary bulb on that warm night in Romania, that gypsy said maybe he wasn't such a bad horse after all.

When I left in the morning he was grooming him all by himself and I handed the horse some plums.

The gypsy said they'd choke him so I tried to get across to him that horses are pretty clever, that his was no exception, that he'd spit the stones out, and when I rode away I saw the gypsy counting.

You know, I love horses, I really do.

The Road to Bābāiṭa

There's a thing stallions do and it's called flehmen. I don't know why it's called flehmen. I don't know what sort of word it is. I don't know why the bloke who invented it invented it. I don't know why he didn't invent another word instead of flehmen which sounds better. But anyway, it's when a horse pulls his top lip up and stretches his neck. Mostly stallions do it, but sometimes other horses do it, though they're not supposed to. Bulls do it too. So did Karo. The whole time. But then Karo used to be a stallion before they chopped his balls off, so he was allowed to do it.

Karo was pretty strange really. He did this flehmen thing a lot, but he was just about the most un-flappable horse in the world. It was as if he was living on another plane. When anything happened to him, it was as if it didn't really matter, and he'd let it wash over him and he'd be unruffled. Except for cranes – cranes always ruffled him. I don't know why Karo was so anti-cranes.

Anyway, he was both friendly and remote: sort of like he wasn't really there.

I thought maybe he was lonely.

He was always very keen to meet other horses, very keen, which made me feel he needed a friend, and here he was, going along with me all alone and I thought he must be lonely. But he didn't have to be lonely much longer because André who came out to Romania, André and I bought him another horse, and she a bruiser. She was called Puşa and she was a real case.

After we left the gypsy and his stallion, we went out the back way from Giurgiu past all these great pipes running all over the place, rusty and huge. Don't ask me what was in them, except in one place there was a big leak and everything round the leak was dead. They weren't the first

72

pipes I'd seen. Communist countries specialise in huge pipes. The ones I saw in Bulgaria were big switchback jobs with loops over the road. They were in Byala. Byala was a real twenty-four carat dump. Never go there. A fellow in Byala said something I won't forget though. He said communism taught him two things:

'to drink' – and he had a big swig on a bottle of raki just to show he could, then he wiped his mouth with the back of his hand and said,

'and steal.'

Just beyond these pipes were some tall wigwam things where other gypsies hung out but we didn't stop to jaw with them because otherwise we'd just be stopping the whole time. They were peculiar though, those wigwams: very tall: just like red Indians' tents and made of hide. Really I suppose we should have stopped and jawed with the gypsies because there were dozens of horses and Karo could have gone to meet them and not been lonely and I could have found out about these wigwams, but we didn't stop, we went on up this dirt road.

That road wound on round a corner up a bit of a rise and I thought there would be lots of little hills everywhere, like the Cotswolds, but when we got round that corner we hit the plain.

That was some plain.

Altogether, including when André came out, we were riding that plain for two weeks.

Of course Karo and I didn't know how big it was at first, and we were quite glad to be on it because once you're on a plain you go a long way quickly. You can push your average of thirty or forty kilometres a day up to fifty and you won't tire the horse. I walk a lot anyway, and it's easy going along on the plain but the road we were on was gritty and hard on your feet.

Acacias had been planted all the way along that road and we were on it all day. A flight of bee-eaters came along with us for mile after mile, just skimming the treetops: they're spectacular colours, bee-eaters. And in the treetops cicadas were rasping out this high-pitched ringing, the noise they make only when it's really hot. Funny how that noise seems to make it feel even hotter, as if it gave sound to the heat. I heard golden orioles too, way off, but you don't see them: they're shy birds. And not one car came by.

What I found was this: I found I liked Romania straight away. There was something in the earth, something in the trees and the fields, and in that plain: it was like a great big spirit, warm and strong and smiling. Even though I was still a bit nervous because I kept on thinking how everyone said I'd be mugged, when we stopped for our lunchtime hole-up, this character came over to us and he brought me bread and water and raki – they call it ţuica – and another fellow brought barley for Karo.

We slept under a tree that night, Karo and me, and I remember the moon. I remember it really well because it was just like the moon back in Bulgaria when Little Pink was showing off with his hobbles and I thought about him. I thought about him a lot actually, and still do. He was a good horse, Little Pink.

I remember the next day too because that was the first time I saw Romanian village architecture and thought it marvellous. That they should have built such joyful little houses while under Çeauçescu's heel signalled to me a people with real spine.

In that village street there was an old well with a big wheel handle for pulling up the water. The houses were laddered along the road; each one was different. They were like goblins' houses, blues and reds and greens, mauves and yellow. Each one had a different style but mostly they were colonnaded like little palaces and the columns were decorated, some even having stiff leaf foliage like our cathedrals, and the workmanship was painstaking and intricate. One house, much bigger than the others, had a fairy pointed roof, and columns on two floors. It was painted violet and mauve. You wouldn't believe it. The colours should have been a disaster but somehow they worked and it was quite a place.

Of course there was nothing much in the shops but they were better stocked and run than many Bulgarian ones and all the gardens were full of flowers and pigs and cows and horses, hundreds of horses with their green and yellow carts and everyone wanted to know what Karo and I thought we were doing.

I was taking a snap of a house when a woman came over to me and led Karo and me down a path to the collective, and once again Karo got barley and I got whatever was going. I hadn't asked.

There were big barns in that collective, great wooden barns, granaries, and I swear to you they were out of the Bible.

They had tractors, of course, but they were old. Mostly the work was done by horse – except for the combining which was getting underway – but even the grain was carted from the field to the granary by horse, then shovelled by women.

I looked inside the granary. The air was black with barley dust. Barley dust is filthy tack to handle.

'*Miseria!*' the women cried out, eyes streaming, but they shovelled on '*Miseria!*'

I know that they meant: I've shovelled barley, plenty of it. I never want to shovel it again.

Those Romanians worked. All day. They worked in the heat of the day and they worked at dawn. They worked right up to the last light of day and some of them even worked at night. If Çeauçescu was one big thief, if he stole everything he could, he was fortunate to have had a people to rob who are as industrious and tough as the Romanians. And they're proud: and you can't stop them working. Whereas in Bulgaria anyone was prepared to drop everything and spend the rest of the day with you – which was kind – the Romanians put their work first. I discovered that in Bābāiţa, where I pitched up a day or so later. It was midday and both Karo and I were boiled.

I asked in the collective if I could buy some lucerne. Someone went off to get the Domnul Ingineer.

The Domnul Ingineer was called Gheorghe Martinescu and he was quite a guy.

The Bandit

The first thing you see of Bābāiţa is the water tower. So you're on your pony plodding along somewhere out in the plain and the distance is screwed up in heat shimmer, the trees are all stippled like watercolour trees, smudged and dancing, then you see a silvery onion-shape through them and that's the water tower. Every village has one.

It takes forever to get to them.

Somehow the heat winds the distance up and you think they're closer than they are. Sometimes it can take nearly half a day to get to them. The plains are deceptive like that.

And every village lies in a buckle of land, as if some giant has got hold of the plain and wrung it out and dumped it back with this big twist in it and in the twist there'll be a stream.

There was a stream in Bābāiţa. Quite a big one. It had turned marshy when I got there, but that marsh went down through the twist and came out in a big reservoir, the barrage. Karo and I got to swim in the barrage every day.

My first night in Bābāiţa I spent in the home of Gheorghe Martinescu, but we ate in a house you would have sworn was pure pixie. And the colours! It was all bright red tapestries, and cloths draped over everything, full of wild patterns, yellows and pinks and blues and on the wall was a crucifix and beside this a cupboard with crockery, all knobbled and extraordinary with filled-in handles as if the fingers of the owners were too short to put through them. It smelled of napthalene and soap and everything sparkled. There were dolls and porcelain, pots and pottery standing in dark corners on little bright-painted stands. The outside of the house was blue and green with silver pillars and if you peered in through the window it was like the home of some little pixie torn somewhere between the pagan and the pious, and it was shared by two old men. They were brothers and a sadder pair of old men you'd never meet. For all the brightness and joy in that little house they had a sadness about them which you could feel as if the air around them

76

was black with it. I don't know why they were so sad. One of them even burst into tears while we were eating and it put a peculiar atmosphere on everything and it made me light-headed and swimmy.

The meal they gave us – that's Gheorghe Martinescu and Sandu and the farm president and me – was chicken grilled on corn cobs with garlic crushed and served in a bowl with tomatoes, and bread. And țuica.

'*No rok!*' the old boys moaned, and we all touched glasses.

'*No rok!*' Gheorghe clinked back and his eyes glittered.

'*No rok!*' said Sandu. Good luck.

Gheorghe lived in Orbeasca a little way from Bābāiṭa, and he was responsible for setting out the agricultural policy for the whole collective. I wanted to know about collectives and Gheorghe told me. The one at Bābāiṭa is 1,730 hectares. They were growing 600 hectares of triticale – pasta wheat: it doesn't blow and you can feed it to horses, they love it – 300 hectares of maize, 30 hectares of root crops, 100 hectares of lucerne and 70 hectares of *pl. Juraj*, [and I don't know what that is because I can't read my notes!].

Gheorghe was the Domnul Ingineer, as I said. Domnul is Romanian for Mr and Ingineer means he went to university and trained especially for the job. All the way through Romania you'll find Domnul Ingineers. They are referred to by their titles and they're a well-educated lot. Gheorghe spoke French and his knowledge of Latin was a sight better than mine. He knew the Latin for everything. When explaining what they grew, he said it in Latin: the trees he pointed out – *quercus robur, fagus sylvatica* – it was extraordinary. The cows, if he forgot his French, were *bovis*, the sheep *ovis*, the wheat *triticum*, the maize *zea mais*. We understood each other.

Gheorghe was not a big man in stature and he had great charm. His face was full of character, but every time he wanted to say something to you he gave you a good prod. Prod, prod, prod. '*Chirimee, voulez-vous visitez les bovis?*'

'*Ah, oui, merci Gheorghe.*'

Prod, prod, prod. '*Chirimee, desirez-vous pour dejeuner du porcus?*'

'*Ah, merci Gheorghe, avez vous du porcus* without fat?'

'*Quoi?*'

'*Porcus minima?*'

'*Quoi?*'

'Skinny *malinki* longlegs *porcus, connaissez-vous?*'

'*Skinn ...? Non. Nous n'avons pas cette animal.*'

I tried my Romanian.

'*Eu vreau sa cumpar an altro cai.*' I want to buy another horse.

'*Pour manger?*'

'*Non! Non! Pour mon ami qui arrive d'Angleterre any minute now.*'

'*Aha! Unul altra cai! Bun! 20,000 lei.*'

Karo was living in the collective being looked after by Tudor, the vet, a socking great bloke with a turkey-cock-red complexion and a cupboard full of horrific wine. Tudor was always smiling and joking and bossing everyone about. He took charge of Karo. Karo got a lot to eat. Tudor fixed that. Karo was pretty pleased. I looked at the farm horses to see if maybe I could buy one, but they were ropey. Tudor saw the look I gave them.

'*Antehelimtic nimic!*' he said.

'*Medicament nimic!*' he cried and threw open his cupboard. I looked at the wine. He shrugged his shoulders.

'Anaesthetic,' he groaned pulling a face and reaching for a bottle. We drank the anaesthetic.

'*Disinfecsion!*' he said and tried another. We drank from urine sampling jars.

I don't know why it was, but I fell for Bābāiţa, and it really isn't much of a place. If you went through in a car you'd go through in a car, but I got to know it. I got to know those low red pantile-roofed farm buildings, I got to know the granaries where the women shovelled the wheat, and the ricks where they hand-stacked tons of loose hay and green oats. I got to know the store where the women loaded two-hundredweight bags of fertiliser onto horse carts and I got to know the machinery shed where the blokes held together and kept running a fleet of 35 ancient combines.

I got to know the well up in the farm and the place they brewed up the țuica, the shed where they milked the cows, I tasted the milk, warm and buttery, a pint of milk to half a pint of flies. I went out in the mornings with the old boys on their carts or rode out alongside them with Karo for exercise and sat with them beneath the shade of the tall poplars when they ate. I drank their warm fly-buzzed beer and pitched lucerne with them by the forkful in the hot winds that whipped in off the plain. I went out with them in the harvest as the combines groaned, shuffling grain, as belts slapped, augers squealed and those clattering old machines roared all day, every day, night and day until the wheat was cut. I sat with the women on piles of corn out in the sun, went with Sandu and Gheorghe to see the irrigation kit, held together with wire and welding, the pumps squeezing their best from machines we in the West would have slung out years ago. In the workshops, tractors were hauled in, bearings shot, axles bust, and those blokes set to in the heat and made new ones.

The Romanians know how to work, and if I was going to put any money into Eastern Europe, I'd put it in Romania. I left a piece of my heart in Bābāița.

Because he lived closer to Karo I moved in with Sandu and his family. It was fine living with Sandu except for his bog.

I was used to the abluting arrangements in Bulgaria and they were different. There are no flushing lavatories anywhere except in the hotels and if you can stomach those you're halfway there. All the facilities otherwise were long-drop or not-so-long-drop. And the thing that kept occurring to me was there were all these not-so-long-drops in every garden and there were all these pigs and their deposits, and the cows and their offerings, and the chickens and what they provide, and the not-so-long-drop, and the well. Sandu's system beat the lot. It was a real gut-curdler, his bog was. It took a lot of hacking first thing in the morning. And it was an awkward place to get to. Like everyone, Sandu had a pair of dogs chained up in his garden who'd yowl their heads off every night all night, and they also guarded this grim citadel. God knows why. Who the hell was going to pinch his bog? If somebody was going to pinch Sandu's bog they needed serious counselling. It was a horror. So in the morning you didn't want to be barefoot, because you had to try and get past this mad dog, then this other mad dog, and wade through the turkey doo-dah, past the pigs and their nightly additions, and not step on the ducks and all they managed to supply and mind the chicks and their black and white heaps, and when you'd done all that you had to watch it because his bog was wobbly and the chances of going for a purler down it were high and some dirty blighter round there wasn't that good a shot.

Which reminds me: I had a horse once called Rooster's Target. He was a buckskin Appaloosa, and flecked. He was well named.

And another thing: I once was called on to make the announcements on sports day at school. They'd just had these whacking great loud hailers fitted. One of the competitions was the shot-put. I had to say 'Would all the competitors for the shot-put please report to the shot-pit.'

I got it wrong.

Anyway, I moved in with Sandu and Sandu was a bear of a man with a big tum which hung out of his shirt and over his pants like a roll of old dough. He'd scratch it every now and then, fish a chunk of dirt out of his belly button and flick it about and all the while he'd be grinning with this big glad grin and there wasn't an inch of malice in that man though everyone called him The Bandit.

Sandu had straight black hair which flopped in front of his eyes and when he smiled you could see the dark tartar stuck between his bottom teeth. Ten years or so ago he was a wrestler. Which was not hard to spot. Everybody respected him and I got to learn the reason.

When Çeauçescu was in power – and he had been, only eight months before I got there – every village was rationed, and people were allowed half a loaf a day. Everyone kept their animals, but as often as not the securitate would suddenly swoop in and spoil a garden for the hell of it or confiscate livestock for the hell of it, or suddenly commandeer a whole village's livestock and that would be that. Now the reason Sandu was called The Bandit was because he'd go out at night and pinch stock from the collectives, butcher them and deliver the meat to the old people who couldn't cope. He was a kind of Robin Hood. If he'd been caught he'd have disappeared. Plenty of people disappeared under Çeauçescu. Luckily no one informed on him. The securitate used the lever of instant imprisonment against anyone who didn't inform and so built up a network of terrorised civilians living in constant fear of their lives and in fear of their friends.

Nobody forgot what Sandu had been. Nobody.

He talked about what it was like under Çeauçescu. How they were always hungry, how Çeauçescu hogged the television every night for three hours, what lies he peddled about production, what a megalomaniac madman they saw him as and how when he was shot it was too good for him and he should have been skinned, piece by piece, because that was all he deserved, all he would have understood. Sandu talked about Çeauçescu's son, how he fancied this little ballet dancer girl who was only seventeen and she wouldn't let him near her so he had her fingernails torn out – just three years ago. To have spoken to a foreigner meant arrest: to have spoken out at all meant you vanished. Children were swiped off the streets and seconded into the securitate but mostly, the securitate were orphans and I was to hear a terrible story some time later from a man who fought at Timişoara, a man called Ursa, and a gentler fellow you'd never meet, but he shot children – there being a great deal more to this story.

So I lived with Sandu and his ever-patient wife who slaved away doing everything while we gorged ourselves on their poultry. Then she did the clearing up and cleaning up, and off we'd drift in his jeep while she stayed at home and prepared the next round and we'd come back hours later to be fed again. But it's like that in Eastern Europe. The blokes always eat alone and the women do the graft. It's like that all the way to West Germany. The blokes do nothing in the houses, they don't lift a finger.

I could get to like it.

Gheorghe came round for supper every night, we enjoyed the craic, and I tried to get a grip of what was going on. It seemed the collective was going to be split up between the workers. There were five hundred workers. I told Gheorghe it sounded like financial suicide. He asked me to explain about western business methods. He asked the wrong guy. I've got about as much business acumen as your proverbial mud brick. But I tried and we had a rowdy conversation in French, Italian, Romanian and Latin, with jottings and profit and loss accounts, and I tried to show him what a balance sheet looked like, but couldn't quite remember, especially after half a bottle of ţuica.

Prod, prod, prod ... 'Fixed costs? What are those? Credit? Credit? Who from? Profit and Loss? For whom? What does profit do? Whom for? When? No, we'll go on as we are, we understand that.'

'But that's not progress, that's survival!'

Prod, prod, prod ... 'Yes, but it's a lot better than last year. Wages have doubled! The pensioners get more! We can eat! Look at all this food!'

'But Illeascu's just bought you! Look, all he's doing is greasing up to you! He wants you to divide up the collective because it perpetuates the system!'

Prod, prod, prod ... 'No *rok!*' Clang!

Prod, prod, prod . . . 'When do you want to buy this other horse?'

'What about Illeascu?'

Prod, prod, prod ... 'There's a horse for sale near here.'

'Is there? Let's go and see it.'

Prod, prod, prod ... 'What about a joint venture? Why don't you get some English companies to help us? Why don't you invite us to England?'

'Consider it done.'

Prod, prod, prod ... 'No *rok!*' Clang!

'Let's send them some presents!'

'Who?'

'The English companies who will invest here. What do they like – pigs?'

'Yeah! Grand idea! Send Maggie Thatcher a wad of pork fat.'

They were great those two guys: really great.

Submerged

Karo was central to everything in all this time and I spent hours and hours with him. He was getting pretty tubby even though I exercised him every day and took him swimming. I enjoyed swimming him and was sure he enjoyed it too, because we'd plunge into the water and do a big circle, then he'd wade out all glossy and wet and roar around like a madman screaming his head off at the other horses before settling down to graze. The water kept him clean and in those temperatures the best thing you can do for a horse is keep him clean. And the reason I think he yelled his head off at the other horses was because he was still a bit lonely.

I nearly lost him one day down in the barrage when I was trying to cross the stream where it turned into the river. It was thick with weeds but I thought Karo could wade through them and we'd get to the other side, maybe twenty yards or so. In the middle he suddenly gave up. He just wouldn't go on and so I slid off his back and then realized he was slipping under the water and his hind legs were right underneath him.

I bellowed in his ear and shouted and hollered; he pulled himself together, got going again and we reached the other side in one big froth but if I hadn't screamed at him I think he would just have slipped beneath the water and that would have been that. No more Karo! Then on the other side I took him into the barrage and swam him again, and he got out and threw himself round like a madman, so it didn't seem to do him any harm.

André and Puşa

André came out.

Gheorghe, Sandu and I went to get him from Bucharest. We drove there. A long hot drive across the plain where in the distance the nodding oil wells nodded and buffaloes toiled in the shafts of carts out in the sun.

When we arrived in Bucharest I hadn't realised how big a deal the shoot-out with the securitate had been. There are a lot of bullet holes in Bucharest, a lot of wreaths. Of course I'd seen the revolution played out on television, along with the rest of the world, but you don't get any idea of the terror of it all from the television, nor any sense of scale. I was to get to know the scale later on, from Ursa. There was fighting in Arad too and Sibiu. These people were going to have the securitate out and they went about it with gusto.

Bucharest is a big university town and was pretty lawless when we were there; talk of trouble with gypsies, murder, rape, theft on a big scale. The miners had just been in town beating up students and it was the students who stood against Çeauçescu: it's a bit hard trying to fathom out who's on whose side.

The traffic problem was a nightmare too and there were cars all over the place taking no notice of traffic signs.

If Bucharest was once called the Little Paris of the East, maybe it will be again one day, but I saw it as a dangerous and grimy city, locked in the broken legacy of a madman.

Mike Brown, the Second Military Attaché at the British Embassy met André from the airport and helped get us together. He was given huge boxes of peaches by Gheorghe and Sandu; as they had been loading them into the jeep in Bābāiţa, Gheorghe had said 'Must make a good impression.' He was like that, Gheorghe.

And we visited the dollar shop, not under duress, but to get essential provisions: Kent cigarettes.

A packet of Kent cigarettes works wonders in Romania, and were retailing on the black market at a hundred lei. If I hadn't got Kent cigarettes, I'd still be there. I wonder if Kent will send me some money for all this free advertising? I could do with it. I didn't buy Kent cigarettes for any other reason than to bribe, and that's the way things work out there.

We got whisky too, and pif-paf. Pif-paf is a bit of a godsend because in Romania there's a bit of a fly problem.

Then we all waved good-bye to Mike Brown and Teresa, his wife, who posted films and stuff back to the UK for me, and he produced another official embassy letter explaining the nature of the ride.

On the way back to Bābăiţa we went past one of Çeauçescu's bulldozed villages and saw the empty faces of the people forced to live lives they cannot possibly survive in high rise blocks. We went over the vast canal which Çeauçescu ordered to be built from the Danube to Bucharest, lined in white marbleize. It's vast: otherworldly: something from dreams, nightmares.

André had been in Bucharest for a day or two and went to see Çeauçescu's palace. 'Makes Buck' House look like the size of a privy,' he said. 'Size! What? Gawd, shouldn't like the light bill.'

It was a long hot drive back to Bābăiţa under the afternoon sun, while out in the plain heat played with distant lines of poplar and André yammered on about his goats and this horse called Falcon, and the Met and his saddlery and his wife, and how he was already missing his little 'uns, and had I bought another horse yet, and so now we'd got two saddles and one horse, and had I thought about buying a chariot, and how much was beer? Sweat was running off us.

And he took to Bābăiţa immediately. I wondered what he'd make of Sandu's bog. He came out checking his feet. 'Phew,' he said. 'You don't want to make any mistakes in there. What's for dinner?'

'Pork fat.'

'Sounds nice, anything with it?'

'More pork fat.'

'Oh, good. Where am I dossing?'

And so here he was in Romania, and I'd been looking forward to seeing him. He arrived with saddle, headcollar bridles, bits, saddle-bags – he made mine – and everything else a travelling cowboy wants, including a curly pipe, curly brimmed blue cowboy hat and a pile of photographs of his 'young 'uns.' He showed them around.

Sandu shook his head.

'What's the problem?' he showed them to Gheorghe, who was pulling away on this curly pipe. Gheorghe shook his head.

'What's the matter?' André asked again.

'They're blonde, André.'

'Well?' 'You're not blonde, André.'

'Well tell 'em my Mrs is blonde! *You* tell 'em, tell 'em she's blonde! Tell 'em my grandmother was a gypsy! Go on! Tell 'em!'

They'd never have guessed, André, really they wouldn't.

'Well, what have they got to barter? Where's this horse?'

And there was a girl he liked and she was called Florenza, but she was married and he was married, and they kept apart.

Being married didn't prevent him from coming to Romania, though in fact I think his wife was quite keen.

'No, you go off and enjoy yourself. How long are you going to be away? Oh, that's nice.'

Now André is taller than me and has black hair and brown eyes – you must've gathered. He's got a dragoon moustache and wandered around Bābāiţa in a pair of sawn-off jeans, no shirt, his boots, and this battered floppy blue felt hat, all the while smoking his curly pipe, and they didn't know what to make of André. André's a Bubear and his forbears were Bubears and lived in France. Once he showed me a grimy photograph of his old man who'd been in the Foreign Legion, but died when André was very small. He's a horseman, André, having served with the Blues and Royals, household cavalry and is now – unless he's got the sack – master saddler for the Metropolitan Police.

'What about a surcingle?' he says. 'Surely you could do with a new surcingle?' You notice he's eyeing up your chainsaw.

'No, bugger off Bubear, I've got a hundred surcingles. And I like my chainsaw.'

'What about a new old saddle then?' You move your chainsaw out of sight.

'What about a new pair of chaps? Or another hat? Hat bands? Belts?' So André billeted in the room beside mine in Sand's house and we ate all Sandu's poultry and pork fat and swam Karo in the reservoir, walked one end of Băbăiţa to the other, drifted across the plain to Orbeasca and all the time André was falling for Romania, just as I had.

But the one thing he didn't take to easily was breakfast. Breakfast in Romania is different to ours.

Sometimes there isn't any. Quite often, actually.

And sometimes it's just ţuica, which at seven in the morning takes a bit of downing.

'*No rok!*' they'd bawl and fill your tumbler to overflowing.

'*Sanatate!*' Good Health!

'*No rok.*' André groaned as he rolled his glass round in his hand looking for somewhere to ditch it.

'*No rok!*' they clinked guzzling theirs, smacking him on the back, waiting for him to finish so they could charge his glass again. And when they had, they dug what was left over from last night's supper, either hot or cold, or sort of tepid, but with a liberal sprinkling of flies and more ţuica. If wildly lucky, you got herb tea in the mornings and that was very good. But you needed to be lucky. The days were hot. The smell of earth and dust and cows filled the village. The air was heavy with grain dust pulled in from the plain on hot dry winds.

The harvest was roaring full swing and Gheorghe and Sandu spent long hours out in the fields, driving through them by night keeping an eye out for theft, because theft was commonplace. There's nowhere for anyone to grow their own bit of grain for straw and it was straw that disappeared.

Ceauçescu's system pinched every bit of land and there's not an inch of Romania which is not used in some way. The government took all the agricultural produce and left its people to feed themselves. This is common enough throughout the Eastern Bloc.

Where did all this produce go? I know what a decent field of wheat looks like, or a goodish stand of corn. I'd ridden through millions of tons of the stuff in Bulgaria alone. Where's it all gone? The same question pops up in Romania: where did it all go? If it went for export, as apparently it did, and judging by Ceauçescu's extravagances we know how much the money was squandered, what happened to it in Bulgaria? Clearly, it never got anywhere near the people who were left to feed themselves: hence the man in Byala and what communism taught him.

There's a joke they tell in Romania. A prize sow farrowed nine piglets. Çeauçescu was told she'd farrowed eleven. Fine, he said, export nine, and keep the rest for home consumption.

We'd been looking for horses as the days rolled by, then one evening Gheorghe took us to a small village called Merişan, and that's where we saw her.

We'd seen other horses, but none like her.

She cast a spell over us: bewitched us; it was that neat little muzzle and that broad forehead; it was the look in her eye – she had a share of brains, this one; it was those little short cannons to the front and big long shannons to the rear and her colouring – sometimes she was black and sometimes she was gold. She had a hogged mane.

But that head! That convex nasal bone and those eyes; this was patrician elegance in some very peculiar horse.

'*Che raca?*'

'Mongolese,' the man said. I saw André grin.

We split our dollars, changed them on the black market, shoved in half apiece and we'd bought another horse.

The man counted. The pile of lei was enormous. He was happy. He smiled. Out came the ţuica.

'*No rok!*'

A piece of her mane was cut and the man dithered about digging out luck money for us, a coin, as a memento, but his eyes were on the pile of lei. We'd paid well in his terms – as a tourist you do – but in ours she was cheap: 400 dollars.

'And there's something else ...' the man pointed ... 'she's two horses, one small short Mongolese inside.'

She was pregnant.

André jumped in the bloke's cart and the mare was tied alongside. Everybody had to wait impatiently while the fellah got his hat. Hangers-on were excited: money had changed hands, the Englishmen had gone mad and bought a wild horse. The fellah picked up the reins then handed them to André, and André drove those horses to Bābāiţa through the poplars on the dirt road, just above the barrage as the sun set behind him.

Driving back with Gheorghe in the jeep I had a chance to see the mare properly and watched her move, and saw she spent most of her time airborne. She had what is called by some horse copers 'the movement'.

When he got back to Bābāiţa, André was beaming.

'She can kick an' all!'

'What's her name, André?'

'Pusher, that's how you say it, but you spell it Puşa.'

Puşa

André snores.

My room was about ten feet from his and I heard him loud and clear.

He said I snored.

That night I didn't hear him snore at all. I think he must have been thinking about that mare. Or Florenza. But anyway if he was thinking about that mare, I wouldn't have blamed him because she was some fancy pony. I've never seen one like her. She was pretty savage back in Merişan: a biter, the bloke said. Maybe she bit him, she was certainly marish, but I expect she bit him for a reason: she had whip weals all over. And one way and another Puşa covered roughly three thousand kilometres and I knew her to bite once only and that was because she was shut in a stable when she wanted to be outside and I didn't blame her for that.

But she bit Karo. Karo got bitten to bits. And though she bit him, she loved him.

She loved Karo: adored him, wouldn't let him out of her sight, not as horses normally do, but with a kind of lunatic terror, fear that he might disappear altogether or something. She stuck with him like putty to wool. So Karo wasn't lonely any more because he had Puşa, but I bet there were times when he wished he didn't have her, because she was some female, Puşa. She gave him the battering of his life every now and then, and bit the poor fellow half to pieces for nothing, and she was a little harridan to him the first time André and I went up to the farm and tried her with a saddle.

André mounted her carefully and she knew he wasn't going to hit her so she was quiet. He kept his feet out of the stirrups because if she was going to have a go he didn't want to get dragged. But she didn't. Then we took both horses down to the barrage and we swam them right out into the water so everything was submerged except their heads, and if you ever need to make a horse, that's how you do it. She was made in thirty seconds and never fussed again. It's the best way I know of making a horse into a rider.

When they'd dried off we walked them back to the village, past the water buffaloes in the bulrushes and the old men with their donkeys up in the maize and the children watching over the water buffaloes, and the sun was beating down and we had our shirts off. And in that moment, André suddenly took a big interest in everything around him. I saw it happen.

He pointed to the water buffaloes, to the old boy with the flat hat and the tiny donkey. He pointed back to the barrage and said the fishermen had arrived, that the trees were looking tired from the heat and had I seen the fireflies last night? He pointed up to the place where Florenza had talked to him first when we were out with the combines, and over to the black old shed where they brewed up the ţuica. He did all this because he was doing what he came out to do, what he'd set his heart on; he had, in part, achieved what he wanted and there's nothing in the world that'll lift your spirit as quick and high as that.

He groomed Puşa till she shone. He made her a new headcollar bridle out of soft cotton. He fitted that saddle until it was perfect, and while he did this I left him and went off with Gheorghe and Sandu because that was to be our last night in Bābāiţa and they were going to give us a send off.

Sandu drove off the way I'd first arrived on Karo and we wound down into this bit of a village to a rambly bar and he bought a barrel of beer. The beer in Romania is always warm, and the bars aren't that fussed about hygiene and so usually you get a lot of flies to your jam-jar full, or whatever it is, but Sandu said, 'For you, *fratre mio*, tonight the beer will be cold.'

Out the back of this bar was a low hut, long and thatched. There were no walls. It was just roof. We went towards it carrying big plastic bags and I had no idea what the plan was.

Sandu winkled the door of the shed open as I stood there sweating.

Inside was a pit, and it was covered in straw. Sandu got down into the pit – no great depth, maybe a yard or two, and he scraped the straw away.

The temperature outside must have been ninety. Inside the hut it must have been sixty. Sandu drove a pick-axe through the last bit of straw, then bent down, grabbed what he'd smashed and handed it to me.

'For you, *fratre mio*, tonight the beer will be cold.'
'Ice! How does it get here?'
'Winter. It's cold here in the winter.'
'How long does it last?'
'Until next winter.'
That night, the beer was cold.

Everyone came to the party. The mayor, he of the pork-pie hat and the big hangover: he who slugged white wine by the bottleful at seven in the morning bleary-eyed in his office, pushing bits of paper round, then reached for the bottle again; he was a nice man, with a big soft, far-away look. His wife cooked a crushed maize dish that sat in my belly for a fortnight solid. Gheorghe, Sandu, the local policeman, the mechanics, the farm president – all of them.

It was very hard leaving Bābāiţa.

Sandu is my brother as Gheorghe Martinescu is my brother, as that village was my home and where, for the two weeks I spent there, I knew nothing but happiness, met the hand of kindness and left, with André, on horseback, stuck for words.

As we rode out the gates of the farm, the only golden oriole I ever saw landed in an apple tree beside us.

One Hot Slog

We walked in silence for hours, just walking the horses, in the heat, then got off, then on again. André was very careful of Puşa's back. He's like me and won't mount a horse the same side twice. You just can't afford to do it when you're travelling with them. You can't just go on pulling away at one side of the saddle, on one side of the horse's back the whole time. I don't know why people will insist on mounting one side anyway. What for? Why? Someone once bellowed at me for mounting right leg in and said it was wrong: I told them to tell that to the horse. Strikes me as daft, one side mounting: you're far more likely to damage a back like that than keeping both sides even, keeping leathers even, saddle straight, backs dipped even. No, you mount one side, then the other, get off different sides. None of it's easy with all the clobber on when you're travelling but you don't get sore backs that way. And we soaked the horses' backs the minute the saddles came off, which stops heat bumps. I could bore you to death about backs.

And out on the plain the nodding donkeys bowed and raised their heads and we gazed in silence through the combine-crawling distance, thinking of Bābāiţa.

We pulled up in some tiny patch of green, in some dry, empty village, where a wisp of grass was the only grazing – because roadside grazing is non-existent in Romania. There's little for the wayfaring man.

Though we were both half asleep, half dead from the late night, we were wound-up somehow, and it was hard to settle there, beside that little church and its graveyard. We tethered the horses on long lines, watching Puşa carefully, letting her get the hang of it all, when a man turned up with a pile of lucerne, which we bought for a couple of dollars. A gang of the locals pitched up. They surrounding us, staring. Gradually they drifted off and someone brought some bread: we cadged water. The sky was clear, cool and clear.

We flung down our flea bags on top of numnahs while the horses tucked into the lucerne, and I was looking forward to a long night's sleep. Another likely fellow turned up on a tractor. He hung round considering something, chewing the end of his thumb all the while and staring. You could almost feel thoughts going through his mind. He was dreaming up some way of entertaining us, these two peculiar foreigners with horses, stuck for a night's lodging. A pal of his arrived, they both disappeared and came back clutching a television. Did we know it was the World Cup?

'Oh no,' André sighed.

'*Da! Da!* Moment! Moment! No problemmm!' the fellows piped up enthusiastically. They were excited.

'Oh no! Please! Not *football*! I *loathe* football!'

'*Da! Da!* Football! No problemmm!'

Then another fellow turned up with a long pole, a roll of wire and they rigged that television up to overhead cables and we were forced to watch fuzzy black and white telly at full volume until three in the morning, with this tractor roaring, the horses going bonkers and Italy or someone playing somebody else for hours on end. And the game refused to end . It went on and on and on, with these blokes lolling around all over our bedding, cracking jokes and jawing and laughing and generally having a ripping time, stringing this thing right out to the bitter end.

Finally, finally, it finished but they hung about waffling, doing a post-mortem on every kick before twigging that we were more interested in our bedrolls than any amount of half-understood discussions on the merits of some Italian footballer, so they reluctantly took everything apart and wandered away into the night, kicking imaginary footballs at imaginary team-mates, heading ghost headers and scoring ghost goals.

We waited, anticipating another round of entertainment, but they'd gone. Quietness surged into the vacuum of noise they left behind.

What mighty relief it was: the long-awaited peace. We lay back and closed our eyes. At last quiet crowded round us, the black smothering blanket of night, then thinly, through the darkness came a sound, a very weird sound, a wailing.

Dingy little lights were flickering about in the graveyard.

André sat up, very slowly.

''ell's bells!' he gasped.

'What?' I whispered.

''ell's bells!' he gasped again.

'What?'

'The Undead!' he nearly gagged as he said it.

'*What???*'

'The Undead!' And pointed at flickering lights weaving through the graves.

'It's vampires digging up bodies!'

'For Pete's sake, André!'

We watched these undead wailing around in the graveyard with their candles and shrouds bang in the middle of Dracula country and I can tell you, they fairly spooked the horses and they fairly spooked us and only when the sun came up did we realise it was wailing women mourners and my God, didn't they make a weird noise?

Liliana, Sandu's wife had filled our saddlebags with grub when we left Bābāiţa and for breakfast we'd shared the remains of a duck and a bit more pork fat as the wailing women filed out of the graveyard. They were all huddled and grey and dressed in black and I shouldn't want to spend a night alone there, or with André again, actually, because he put the wind up me. The horses didn't seem to like the wailing women much either and old Karo was very cagey about the whole business because he'd been closest, so I suppose he must have had more of a clue about what was going on, but anyway we all left in a bit of a hurry at sun up.

I've told you how hot it is going along on the plain and how much of a slog it is, and that's exactly how it is. Then the horses just go along with their heads down and the horseflies buzz about them and so they get into this routine of showing you where the flies are and expect you to swat them off, so you go along not really looking where you're going because you're tied up swatting flies.

'I've had enough of staring up Karo's arse,' André said suddenly.

'And I've been counting. He's dumped fifteen times today.'

So André takes the lead for a bit and I have to stare up Puşa's backside, and you go along, staring up your mate's horse's backside, and this way, you cover the miles.

For lunch we hauled up under a spread of trees, hoping for a bit of silence because it doesn't take long for you to get wiped out when you're travelling like that, with little sleep and not much to fill you up except pork fat and duck and all that solid maize concoction which made André say he didn't think he'd ever manage a turn-out ever again.

These trees we were under were a way outside a village and we were just going along on the compass not really knowing where we were, which doesn't matter that much, but the trees were tall and cool, and there was plenty of lucerne for the horses to swipe. André tethered Puşa up and I tethered Karo up and we stretched out half a mile away from each other so as not to wake the other up with snoring, when along slops old Strawberry Nose with his barking mutt. Old Strawberry Nose's got a list of questions and he's pretty blunt with it.

> How much did the horse cost?
> Is that your friend?
> How much did his horse cost?
> Have you got any cigarettes?
> Are you going to stay here?
> How old are you?
> How much was the horse? – again.
> Where did you buy it?
> Do you need that rope?
> Have you got a wife?

I gave old Strawberry Nose the sheepskin jacket Sandu had given me. I gave it to him to make him go away and for two other reasons. First, the temperature was seldom less than a million and a sheepskin jacket was exactly what I didn't need, and secondly, it hadn't been cured so all the bugs in creation were living in it.

Strawberry Nose gave me a kiss for that, then pushed off.

Half an hour later he was back – with his mate, and his barking mutt. Both mutts barked their heads off. And:

Where did I get that jacket?
Have I got another?
How much was the horse?

While I'm on the subject of lists of things we were given on that journey, which, despite protestation, we had forced upon us but had to ditch:

1 sheepskin waistcoat with bugs.
2 ashtrays: 1 tin; 1 glass.
1 pair of antlers.
Approx 21 bottles of raki.
Approx 100lbs of pork fat.
2 tablecloths, very decorative.
1 china dog.
1 small stool.
1 live chicken.
A box of candles.
1 jar of plum jam which bust in my saddlebags.

These articles you may find somewhere on the route we took from Bulgaria to Berlin.

And another thing. My brother Huw once told me what he'd like to do least of all in life would be to stand about outside on a boiling summer's day drinking a lot of cheap red wine, then when really hot and sweaty, so it's all running down your back and you're all claggy under the arms, go in and put a load of really thick old army shirts and stuffy worsted trousers on, and a woolly hat and gloves and then go back out and dig a trench.

I agree. I would hate to do that.

The thing is, riding around in Romania in high summer is a bit like it.

The Good Life

Old crones watched us pass by in open-mouthed silence. Wrinkly grandfathers sitting in the shade of plum trees shrilled at us with shaky voices:

'*As cumperat?*' Have you bought the horses?

You reply with a wave, or a nod and they nod and wave, and slump back, like the old crones.

'*Să trăiţ!*' they salute, and you go on.

Three ducks waddling down the middle of a village road watched us coming towards them. They were confused and turned this way then that, then edged to the side of the road as the horses' feet pounded into the ground beside them, flouring them in dust and I looked down on their confusion, following them as we went by, and saw them standing in a row behind, watching us go, like the old grandfathers sitting in a row watching us go and the old crones sitting beside the grandfathers watching us go and all their faces were the same.

Then you pull up at a well and get off, and the horse sighs and you slacken the girth and wipe the sweat off. André reels the bucket a hundred feet down the well then up and the horses drink, then you drink, and you pour water over the horses' necks and they shake, then you're on the trail again, walking beside your horse, wishing you had a Coke, or a Pepsi, or a Fanta, but you only have water, and sometimes the water is sour. So you reach out for plums and share them with the horses and they slobber plum all over you, and you go on.

Then you're out in the burning heat of the plain trying to find the short way across to the trees maybe five miles away, but there isn't one and that walk is long and hot and when you get to the trees, you're thirsty again and the horses are thirsty again and you can't stop because there's no water, so you go on to the next village and by nightfall you're whacked. Then you have to find somewhere to stay and food for the horses, and food for yourselves and water.

And you usually do.

'The little 'uns are okay: I've fixed up with that old git over there and he's just turned up with a bag of oats, and his mate – the one with the hat, him over there – he's got some lucerne, so they're okay.'

'Have some pork fat, André.'

'Thanks.'

'And a bottle of beer.'

'A bottle? Blimey! Things are looking up. And it's warm, not hot. Cor! What luxury!'

'When did you last wash?'

'Errr ... in Băbăiţa?'

'When was that?'

'Er ... ten days ago?'

'Do I smell as much as you do?'

'Cheers.'

And so you both lean back in the setting sun and watch the village in twilight, and it's peaceful. And here come the water buffalo browsing up the middle of the dirt street with all the cows and sheep and each one peels off into its own gate, and there's a little boy wielding a stick and shouting at the cows. Old men just sit about under the trees.

You realise something then: you see it, feel it, because you can't fail to: you realise they live without stress. No cars, no banks, no mortgage. You do a kind of double-take and look again and there's this fellow's big old Mrs with her big arms standing in the kitchen thumping duff as the cheeks of her bum go chuff-chuffchuff, and there he is, just sitting here beside you drinking ţuica and you see he doesn't give a damn about anything.

'Of course Illeascu's good: we are free! We haven't been free for a long time. Here – take! Eat! Drink! We have plenty!'

And just then, in that moment you catch a glimpse of Utopia and see what the whole thing could have been, because it's soft and easy, they get their pay cheque, they've got their house and their animals and the sun is shining. Maybe they haven't got your dishwasher and refrigerator, or a microwave, or a holiday in Benidorm – but look at what they have got and then, as the sun disappears into the plain, and moths flutter round the oil lamp, you see something about the whole thing that might just have worked, if only ...

It's fleeting, of course – a whole different story in winter – but in that moment I saw what any man on earth would call the good life, and I know plenty of people back home who are trying to earn enough to be able to live like that.

'We've got a double bed again,' André says. 'Your turn to kip on the floor. And stink! Phew! Chicken shit and țuica: everything smells of chicken shit and țuica.' It does and your mood is broken.

'When I get home,' he says, 'I'm going to shoot all my hens and anybody ever gives me țuica or chicken or pork fat again, I'll hang myself.'

Then some old boy beckons you over to him and he does it again because you're not quite sure what he's getting at, but you go and he takes you into a dark old shed, and digs away at the huge pile of rotten straw, and there is his treasure. A phaeton, hidden for forty years – beautifully made – the wheels are shot and full of worm and if he moves it it'll fall to bits: same with that lovely light gig, and the sledge – you should have seen the workmanship on the sledge – a magnificent troika – all reds and greens – buried for forty years. It was more worm than wood. And all those jars and pots, filled with little trinkets, all rotted away.

'Ah,' he says stroking the mudguard of the phaeton, 'maybe they're old, maybe they're rusty, but they're mine. The communists never got these, did they?' and he smiles, and in you go, and out comes the țuica.

'*Sanatate! No rok!*' He' s a canny old boy, and somehow he parts you from a fistful of dollars.

And the next day and the next day you crawl across the plain and then suddenly, and you don't know how it happened, you look around you:

'We're off the plain!'

And you gasp and fill your lungs with air, the cool air of altitude, of trees, and rivers and fields of grass.

The houses are different too, with roofs made of tiny little oak slats.

There's light woodland everywhere and in one valley we rode through, a long dreamy valley where maize was growing in little patches on banks, the smell took me straight back to a childhood of smiling black faces, shambas and horses, of woodsmoke and green mountains – the highlands of Kenya.

We arrived in the foothills of the Carpathians after a long zigzag across country following a rough bearing of 270 degrees north. I was reminded of the Alps and when I rode Gonzo along the valley that goes to Susa, on the Italian side. I remember Rociamelone, the great sacred mountain, and stayed at a place called Cascina Parisio.

Corben was like that. Only in Corben we stayed in the campsite and made a break of it, because it was André's birthday and he'd got presents.

Birthday Kiss

Puşa laid her ears back, stamped her feet and lashed her tail. Everybody scattered.

'Blimey! She even scares me and she's on my side!' André said, running a hand over her face.

'*Bun cai!*' one of the crowd said. Nice horse.

'*As cumperat?*'

'If anybody says *"as cumperat"* again, I'll go mad!' André threw his hands up, and walked off with Puşa.

We'd arrived in Corben, in the foothills of the Carpathians in the middle of the day. The horses needed shoeing and there was a blacksmith; here was a campsite, a river, the village was pretty, the people friendly and once again, we'd been instantly adopted by the leading self-appointed, whose first reaction was to offer us palinka.

'What's palinka?'

'Double ţuica.'

Why does everything have to revolve around alcohol? What about a cup of tea?'

'Two teas, please, miss! – I don't think she understood, André.'

The gang of the curious crept closer again, trying to pat Puşa. Back went the ears.

'God she looks 'orrible! D'you think she'd actually attack?'

'Definitely.'

They fixed us up with a cabin apiece and fodder for the horses. The self-appointed confided, glancing over his shoulder this way and that, slitty eyed and darkly, '*Tsigani* here: your horses will be stolen.'

So we parked them with him that night and paid in the morning and realised the *tsigani* weren't interested in the horses at all, and we'd fallen for the oldest trick in the book. You curse yourself then for being a mug, but what can you do? Maybe he was right the night before, who knows, so you just have to go along with it, and cough up and just make sure you don't get caught again.

Then at nine next morning we took the horses off to the footsmith, a wobbling giant of a man with arms like mutton-leg shotgun cases, huge and polished and brown, and fingers like black puddings, thick and dark with tiny little busted nails stuck on.

He hot shod the horses and if there's one thing we can do to help all horses throughout the world, it's to send them a decent footsmith.

Local smithies don't understand the mechanics of the foot and will cut the foot to fit the shoe, then make shoes with huge calkins so the horse can't straighten its legs. It must be hell to walk. So when André and I asked for shoes without calkins, their first reaction was to say no. That we then had the horse's feet cut right back so the foot was level, allowing for a constant angle from the pastern down, was unheard of, and then to have them hot shod giving long – but flat – heel support to the foot was something they all thought was just plain wrong. Actually, it didn't look too good either, but it was a lot better than what they had had and both horses could straighten their legs.

The smithy was banging the last nail in and André was holding Puşa's foot up, when he announced:

'Hey! It's my birthday! Cor! I should get a kiss! If I don't get a kiss on my birthday, it'll be the first birthday I haven't had a kiss in all my life.'

So after the farriery we had to think about how André was going to get himself kissed and in the meantime took the horses down to the river for a day off in the sunshine. We had a birthday picnic. Pork fat. And as we prodded around with it I wondered who he'd get to kiss him when suddenly he produced birthday presents. He'd carried them all that way, and weren't they a marvellous surprise! To be handed chocolate! A tiny bottle of whisky! Though it was his birthday he celebrated mine as well, and he, his wife and children who'd bought the stuff for us, turned that hot summer's day by the river in Corben into an unforgettable one, just by those presents alone.

We returned to the campsite a few hours later, greeted by a big grinning bear of a bloke called Aurel who'd been celebrating all on his own.

Aurel took to us immediately. Yes, he'd find us a really good place for the horses; come and meet his brother! Would we like to try some of this stuff? Have we been to the bar? Ah! André's birthday! He ought to get a kiss!

'*La mult anni!*' he congratulated. Have we seen the barmaid? She's alright. And we hadn't forgotten his name, Aurel, had we? Aurel! And what Aurel liked was brandy. Yes, brandy! Oh, yes, he was very fond of brandy! They had it in the bar! Look! Oh, yes! That's the one! Ah! He wouldn't mind if he did!

The barmaid poured away, and he smiled the big, benign, friendly, grey-hairy-chested, gormless grin of the three-parts cut.

'*No rok! Sanatate!*'

The barmaid was wearing a kind of Elvis Presley outfit. She wasn't unattractive.

And André got his birthday kiss.

He got a real smacker.

Right on the lips.

He got it from Aurel.

He spent the next twenty minutes spitting.

And Aurel just grinned this big silly grin and everybody was happy.

Except André.

The Carpathians are beautiful, really beautiful. To ride away from Corben in glittering sunlight on fresh horses is something else. Then to go through Curtea de Arges a few miles further on is unforgettable. A more unhappy, down-in-the-dumps patch-on-a-map you'd hardly credit: everybody was drunk, and filthy, the roads dug up, manholes erupting, smoke fogging the sky, the river black.

You realise then the real legacy of communism is squalor.

Maybe the town centre was pretty – we didn't stay. We wound on up through the mountains and stopped by a huge high lake which reminded me of Llyn Brianne in Wales – except there weren't any jets. But the sky was clear, the water like crystal, and we were alone.

I thought about home then, and wanted to see it again. I wanted to see Gonzo and Dolly and Punch and wondered what they were doing just then, while I was thinking about them. Was Gonzo battering gates down? Was Dolly full of laminitis? Was Punch shredding knickers, the inside of Mark's wardrobe? Did he have a belly full of elastic? Had he been popping Mark's children's balloons?

The scenery reminded me a lot of Wales. The rock was like Welsh rock, the mountains rugged, with pine trees and stunted oak, the air fine and feathery and there were buzzards.

But we moved on.

We moved on, staying one night in a huge campsite populated by Eastern Bloc tourists, East Germans in their Trabants, Czechs in their Skodas; there were no speedboats or things like that on the water, just bathers and the sort of things you can do for nothing. There were horses too, loose horses and a fight between Puşa and the local stallion resulted in my getting a hole in my foot, so we stayed, then the next night found ourselves staying in one of Ceauçescu's former shooting lodges – a ridiculous, over-the-top place with a couple of helicopter pads outside. It's got this big balcony right round to lean against with your Kalashnikov and blaze away at the bears.

It's a sort of hotel now, staffed by a posturing posse bunch of twenty-year-olds with an eye for dollars. The one we were landed with was a rheumy-eyed spotty little spiv with a vague louse-bound moustache.

'You want have Nikolai Ceauçescu's private suite?' he whined.

'No.'

'There's a big bed.'

Why were they all determined to get us in bed together?

'Not interested.'

'He stayed here.'

'Don't care.'

We got a room on the ground floor and listened to '... left bum and ipsitum, left by yoooouuu ...' all night while the horses were tethered out in the darkness wondering about the bears.

In the morning the air was clear and we had a better view of things.

'Look at that then,' André said waving an arm. 'Reminds me of The Rockies!'

Round us the mountains crashed and plunged, peaks rose above us straight into cloud, streams darted through valleys while Romanian shepherds and their flocks of sheep-with-one-goat-in ignored the laws of gravity on hillsides opposite.

We could have gone straight over the top, which would have been a bad climb, and after my experience with Karo in the Balkans I wasn't keen on any more mountaineering than was absolutely necessary, so opted for the road, which wasn't busy. A car an hour. Along that road was the tunnel which we'd heard about, though knew nothing of its length, if it was straight or wiggly. We found out.

It was absolutely black. The sunshine on the rock at the tunnel mouth was a blinding contrast. The blackness looked solid.

'I've never been through a tunnel before,' André said, 'on a horse.'

'I have.'

'What's it like?'

'Black.'

'Can't see a thing! What if it's full of bears? Where does it go? Where's the end? How long is it?'

André held Karo's tail, I held Karo's head, Puşa shoved her nose into André's armpit, we walked in and the darkness swallowed us.

'Bluddy 'ell! Don't half miss the little 'uns!'

It's funny how your eyes play tricks in darkness, how things squirm about in front of you, worms. I don't know what they are. I wonder if they squirm around in front of horses' eyes as well?

We burst into sunlight on the far side as though emerging into another world. Astonishingly, there was a fellow selling straw cowboy hats and guess who bought one?

'What about that then?'

It took two more days to get off the Carpathians and it's a long slog all the way down the other side. But to look back on them was good; it's always good to look back on ranges you've passed, and Old Karo had crossed two, Puşa one, and there were more to go. You get a sense of achievement when they're over, and you also get to know the size, exactly what kind of sweat you can build up on a straight seven thousand foot climb, which doesn't sound much – until you have to do it.

On the downland the other side, we moved into different country, a world of grass, and willow, where there was nothing unusual about seeing a couple of blokes out scything a 500-acre field. Water buffalo carts seemed to be the way to get around there: it was like stepping back from the past into a further past.

We were in Transylvania.

His Saddle Slung Over His Shoulder

'There's bugger all in here except rotten jam!'

'Nothing else?'

'More rotten jam!'

'Anything else?' 'umm . . . rotten fish and – bread – I think?' It was a kind of a question which André bawled at the top of his voice. He was inside a village shop. I was hanging on to the horses outside.

'Let's have some rotten fish and bread then,' I shouted back.

We had rotten fish for lunch, with bread, I think.

'This is good,' André said, swallowing a mouthful. We'd lashed up beside a bit of a river where there was fragmites for the horses, and the water was drinkable – just. We had a bottle of ţuica. It was a hot day and flies were buzzing about. We were all in shade and the horses were on top of us. Again.

'You know, I know why they drink ţuica,' André said, spitting out a mouthful of bones. 'It takes the taste of rotten fish mixed with rotten jam away.'

You nod.

'When I get home,' he rambles on looking all thoughtful, now with another mouthful of bones, 'what I'm going to do is tear all the plumbing out of my house,' he stops for a minute and spreads a bit of jam onto his fish butty, spits bones and goes on, 'I'm going to throw out the bath, smash up my bog, dig a hole in the garden and sling up this shed round it – and that'll be the privy. I'll chuck all my clothes out and get a vest with a hole in the front and a pair of filthy old trousers to knock about in. Then I'm going to buy bottles and bottles of ţuica and lurch around pissed all day scratching my arse. I'll invite all these ginks in who come swanning through the village on horses and get my Mrs to do everything for them, wash their clothes, cook and slave away, while them and me loaf about getting plastered. I'll get a Dacia and turn it upside down in my garden and fill it full of chickens, and get a job in the local collective and then I won't suffer from culture shock.'

You stop eating and look at him.

I tell you, he's a bit like living with a strip cartoon, André.

After lunch we gave the bread to the horses, and when they wouldn't eat it, we packed them up and cleared off.

At early evening we wound up on a ferry, hand-operated, with this sunny little pair of rascals running it. They had no shirts on and were lithe and brown, and kept on darting looks at one another. They weren't much in control of that thing and the current was strong: it wasn't a wide river, but it was deep. A hawser connected one bank to the other and the ferry was slung to this at either end. The way they drove it across the river was to pitch one end on to the current and the current would push it.

It felt pretty insecure. Times like that you look at the moorings on the far bank and see they're not a lot more than a couple of old tree stumps that have started to rise from all this pressure. Is it your turn to go for the plunge, you wonder? With your horse, you wonder? The little boys didn't care. They just fiddled with levers and chains and asked us for gum.

Karo was gnawing his bit, the way he does when he's got the wind up. André was hanging on to Puşa.

'How do you get off this thing?'

'Jump.'

'But ... but ...!'

A corner of the ferry thumped in to the bank on the far side:

'Now! Geronimooooooo ...!'

As Karo jumped he kicked the ferry back so André had to get up a bit of a gallop and jumping a shod horse off an iron ferry on to a retreating bank can't be that easy, but I wouldn't know: it wasn't me who had to do it. André knows.

The village on the far bank was a long empty village, with these big old houses and their big old gates, like hacienda gates. Halfway down the road was a domed well, all in fading blue, with a trough beside it. A pair of water buffalo in the shafts of a hay cart were standing there, cudding.

The village houses were single storey, rococo, painted in pastels, with broken shutters slapping about in the breeze. The main street was earth. No one was about. It was like those old films of Transylvania, only more so, and as we rode down the street into the setting sun the only sound was the sound of the horses' hooves.

Then we hear a clatter, and a cart swings round the corner with a young grey pony in the shafts. The guy driving yanks him to a halt when he sees us, pulls back hard on the reins. This is your chance. It's sundown, we need to sort out a night's hole-up.

'*Buna seara!*' you say. Good evening: you've got to butter him up, get in with him. The guy shouts at his pony, and gives you the once over, but you're busy watching the bunch of cows and horses and water buffalo clod-hopping up the street behind him. The cloud of dust they're kicking up is completely gold. All the animals are gold. The low sun dazzles and you squint, turn your pony sideways so you can look at the fellow and smile, and the sun smacks you hard in the face, like a bonfire: it's late in the day, but there's plenty of strength in that sun.

'*Te rag, unde este eel apropiat hotel?*' you ask. Where's a night's billet, if you please? It's your greasing-up act. You know it. André knows it. You know he knows it. You can see him pulling a face, can hear him, 'you slimy git', but you let it go, and he lets it go, because you have to do it.

And the guy opens his hands, and smiles and says, '*Casa mio!*'

This is Romania. I found the Turks hospitable. The Romanians leave them under the carpet.

So we're in. We shove the horses into this courtyard and the fellow pitches a pile of lucerne into another cart and tethers the horses to it. Then he explains about the village, that it's got 80 houses in it, but only four families. Big families, you say. No, he says, you've got the wrong end of the stick: the place is deserted, it's a ghost town, no one lives here anymore, they've all gone to the cities, there are no young people in the villages, they won't stay, they're not going to hang around and count sheep or eggs or mess around with pigs, they want life, towns, music, fun. The village is dying.

There was a girl there: Christina Moldoveanu. She spoke English and spoke it well, was reading it at university, was in the village just for a few days visiting her grandparents. She thought the village beautiful: in those colours and that sunset, it was. It was a step back a couple of hundred years or more. No cars, no streetlights, no tarmac: nothing. It had a peace about it, a great dignified calm you just don't come across in the West, a real old world feel.

We stayed with that man that night and he had this gypsy helper whom he treated like a piece of dirt. He made him sit outside while we ate. No, he couldn't have any țuica, he was a lazy, good-for-nothing slob. All gypsy work was 'slab' they called it, sloppy. And this guy couldn't understand why we tolerate Arabs in the West. *Tsigani*! he called them. *Tsigani scum*!

There was news at the time of Iraq's invasion of Kuwait.

'Why doesn't the West just rub them out?' he asked. 'This Saddam Hussein man is a little Hitler: rub him out now before he thinks he's a big man. He's scum. *Tsigani* scum.'

He was the first man I'd met who'd shown any interest at all in world affairs, and the first one who knew anything of what was going on. His wife was quizzy too. Did we have shops like theirs in England? What was in our shops? Did we have clothes? Or did the women have to make them, like they made theirs? Were the communists in England like Illeascu? He was a good man, Illeascu, he made things change, her pension had gone up, doubled nearly, and everyone was getting a better wage. Pity about the young ones, they won't stay in the country. Who is going to look after the old people? Who is going to farm? There will be no one to farm! She was worked up, frightened, and you could see she viewed her old age with fear because all her family had gone to the town, and now she was there with her ageing husband and they were getting older and older, things were more difficult to do, garden chores more demanding on her old body, while the girl breezed in, and breezed out, and though she might have loved her grandparents, and loved the village, she preferred to be in Bucharest where the action was.

That night it rained and in the morning the village was a swamp. It didn't look so pretty then. You could see how hard it was to live in it then. Sure, it was fine in the sun with the river going past, but in the rain? It must be hell in the winter.

I heard the word '*servos*' there too. It was a greeting. I hadn't heard this word before.

It's a Magyar word; it means hello.

We rode off in light rain and wandered through a valley of ancient villages, just like Colun. Each had two or three churches, a Roman Catholic, Evangelist, and Orthodox. The people were Magyar by root, Romanian speaking. But their allegiances were Hungarian. There'd been plenty of trouble. It was a conversation to be avoided. Nobody wanted that can of worms opened up today, thanks.

One wonderful old dame, to whom we gave three parts of a loaf of hot bread, struggled with us up through a village backstreet and pointed the cross-country route to Sibiu, and that was a ride through high blown country: a ride across heaven: André's last.

He was going home.

A couple of fellows on the road to Sibiu told us of the hippodrome and, prickly heated, at seven that night, we arrived.

Puşa took one look at the place, at every horse in the place and set about it. She booted the buckets out, booted the grooms out, booted the other horses out, booted her stall to bits and then gave Karo a huge kiss.

What a woman.

André and I checked into the hotel and went for a wander round town.

Quite a place, Sibiu.

There are narrow crowded streets with overhanging wood frame buildings, cobbled roads, glorious doorways, and tall gabled houses with fine high eyelet windows in steep roofs. There's a huge great piazza, and the shops were well stocked. You can even slog round a dozen museums if you like to wear yourself right out – really give yourself the heavy-leg. I can't stick museums at any price: they're too dead for me, I find them real killers.

Sibiu's got a bit of a tourist trade and we were dying to meet tourists, but the only foreign car we saw made us angry. It was a Lada. A new green Lada, with Belgian plates, and on the side written in big letters was 'Aid to Romanian Children' – in English. That car was parked outside the most expensive hotel in town. It was parked outside that hotel for the couple of days André and I were in Sibiu and that was a 100 dollar a night hotel. Everything about that hotel was expensive. Now I think I know what I'm saying here and maybe the individual driving that thing had private money, maybe he was being put up by some fat-cat, maybe he was a paid guest in the hotel, maybe there was some other reason, but why did he have to leave it outside the priciest place in town? We weren't the only ones who noticed. André and I had passed orphanages and I went past a couple more after André left, but I didn't see any green Ladas there.

After mooching round town, with nothing else to do we ate a farewell dinner and André said goodbye to Puşa, which took him a long time.

Then he carried his saddle back to the hotel and while I scribbled away he made up a little pack saddle. I didn't want two saddles. I wasn't sure if I'd get Puşa out of Romania because once again all my papers were up the chute – but I was going to try. If things went wrong, I didn't want to find myself stranded at the border with two saddles and one horse.

André cut the girth in half and stitched it to the wither wallets. He folded her saddle blanket so it lay like a saddle, then stitched it up and mounted the wallets on it. There was enough room there for rope, grooming kit, and a night's feed. It was a clever little arrangement, and fixed within the hour. André thought nothing of it, but to me it proved his value as a saddler of ingenuity and clear distinction.

'There we are,' he said. 'It's for Puşa, not for you. First time a pair of 1914 wallets have been converted for a pack-saddle, I'll bet. Everything she needs: no more: no less.'

The last I saw of André was to watch him next morning carrying his saddle over his shoulder on his way out of town. He must have covered six hundred kilometres on it.

He has a wife, children, mortgage, job.

I'd been glad to see him come.

And I was sorry to see him go.

Even if he is like living with a strip cartoon.

And by the way: there's one thing he asked me. He asked me to get Puşa back home. I said I'd try. Karo too.

He's crazy André: he wants Puşa to be godmother to his little daughter.

I hear the Roman Catholic Church has just decreed animals have souls so it's no longer permissible to be cruel to them. Well, well, well.

I know what you mean, André.

Catholic Church decreed animals have souls

Bedfellow

Puşa cried out for André twice next morning and looked round for him, so I shoved the kit on Karo first, but instead of putting the saddlebags on him, put them on her and buttoned her into her new pack. I thought she'd play up and be a bitch, and scream, all that kind of thing, stamp and wriggle and pull away from me when I was up on Karo, so when I mounted, I mounted slowly. But she didn't make any fuss at all, no belly-aching, no booting: just those two calls and it was over and she towed along as sweet as a nut, accepting that André had gone and now we were alone and there was nothing more to say – although she shot a glance back as we rounded the corner from the hippodrome.

We weaved in and out of the cobbled and dirt backstreets of Sibiu as dawn scattered the night sky, and we broke into low rolling country at nine, where the first thing we slapped into was a group of drunken gypsies, one of whom caught Karo by the bridle. This lot were menacing. They had a nasty air about them, a bunch of crooks and that stuck out a mile. There was a big bruiser of a guy in amongst them and he was talking very quietly to another guy and pointing to the horses; they were going to have me off those horses, and were going to have that saddle and those saddle bags and the horses – the lot. These were the type I had not come across, the type the real *tsigani* reject, because they're not gypsies at all, they are *gaje* – anyone who isn't a gypsy – they just pose as gypsies, they're what gypsies call travellers.

And when someone grabs a horse by the bridle, the rider's in trouble: he can't get away: someone else is holding the horse's head, so he's lost. I didn't like the look of the bastard who'd got hold of Karo, I didn't like him one bit. Neither did Karo, but Karo was caught, and the others were closing in.

This guy was shouting about dollars, and cigarettes, and whisky, and then he made to grab Puşa, and Puşa lost no love for him either.

He didn't look what he was doing.

I was holding Puşa by the reins.

Now I didn't know her well at that stage, but I knew her well enough.

I gave her her head, and she laid her ears flat. It's incredible how quick that mare could spin.

Wham! Wham! Wham!

They shouted at us as we trotted away. Two of them ran after us, but we had speed, distance; the get-away is always swift. Looking back, I saw one guy holding his guts squirming about on the road, and I don't care how callous it sounds, but I didn't give a damn. They were lucky she didn't bust them all.

But they must have put a spell on us, because it turned into a rotten day and I got my come-uppance. Karo put himself right behind a fat white mare who gave him both hinds, and I caught it.

I thought she'd broken my leg. She left me writhing around on top of Karo, bawling at him to move, and there he was gawping at this fat white mare like some vacant old vicar staring at an elderly parishioner who'd just come out with a four letter word, having dropped the communion wine, then the mare lashed out again, and I caught it for a second time. Puşa was pulling to get round to give her a boot when Karo shrugged her off, and trogged away gazing into the surrounding scenery like a tour guide from Disneyland, while I clung on to his back hating him, the mare, the day, the weather, travellers, and anything else that sprung to mind. And we didn't leave without another hack from that mare which didn't land.

Cosi fan tutte.

We fetched up in a village about an hour later and I spilled off in a lot of pain. I still had a hole in one foot from the Carpathians and now the other leg was unusable.

Thus was I legless, and treated accordingly.

The man who came over as I lay flat out groaning offered me a glass of vinegary white wine then stood over me belly-aching that I wouldn't drink his wine, and why didn't I stand up? Why do people presume so much? He thought because I was legless I was drunk. I wished I was, and took the glass of vinegar off him, drained it. Then he got the message and gave me another glass of vinegar just in case. I thanked him, loosely, and I don't know how I got back on that horse.

And that night!

Some ten miserable miles or so on, a young fellow popped out of a house in Appoldo de Jos offering me a bed and stabling for the horses – just like that – I hadn't asked.

He was a nice fellow. Very friendly. Very, very friendly. So I collapsed off Karo and we went to his place. He held me under the arm as I limped along. He asked how it happened, and smiled and said everything would be fine.

He was a really friendly guy. The horses were stabled, and I was pushed into a chair with a glassful of the usual.

Then a crowd turned up and with them a little fellah with a new hat and big voice. And this little fellah with a new hat and the big voice talked, and cracked jokes and he thought they were a great hit and everyone yawned as he talked with his big voice and new hat and I was amazed such a big voice could come out of such a little fellah and then everybody drifted off and I was left with him and my host, Dan, his wife and mother, and finally, big voice got the message and drifted off as well.

Dan smiled, offered me some more țuica, and then, seeing I was tired, showed me to my bed. It was a double bed. Very nice, I thought. Just great.

Then I found out I wasn't going to be alone. Which was a bit of a surprise.

Oh God, I thought, oh please God, not that.

But what can you do? There you are in somebody else's place and they've had the decency to put you up for the night, and then comes the pay-off: you get to share your pit: you've got company: they want you to have company. No, no, no, you say: you like to sleep alone. Then Dan strokes you: he's a very friendly guy. You can't just be rude, can you? But, but ... couldn't I share it with his wife? His mother? The girl next door?

And he gave me a big grin and stroked me again, called me darling and asked me if I wanted another țuica.

This was turning into one hell of a day.

Suddenly I wanted to go and check the horses and go and see the little guy with the big voice, or maybe see if there was some place in the village where they mended shoes or made clothes or sold televisions or something – or maybe find someone who could teach me Magyar

– anything! Look, I wasn't a bit tired, not a bit! No, No! I could stay up all night!

No, he cooed, the horses were fine, he was silky; everything was fine and there was nothing in the village, nowhere to go. 'You look very tired,' his eyes were huge. 'Țuica?' My mind was racing: I knew then what it must feel like to be a girl when the predatory male is about to lunge because he's manipulated her into being obliged to him and she's fallen for it.

What about the bloke's wife, for God's sake? What about his mother? Didn't they have a say in this?

I looked at them. They beamed back. My mind was raging with all the stories about travellers winding up in the hands of homo-sex nuts, killers, madmen, people who lured mugs like me into soft white beds then tore into them at the dead of night. Did Dan look like the sort of bloke who'd tear into you at the dead of night? Did he? Those eyes! What kind of eyes were they? Were they the eyes of a failed rapist? Or what? Did he look like a queen? A genuine queen? He looked like a queen, no doubt about it.

What had I done to deserve this? Why did I accept that invitation to stay right out of nowhere! What a mug!

But I was exhausted! My leg was swollen and cobalt-coloured. I couldn't put the other one down – what kind of a scrap was I going to put up? I stayed awake as long as I could with eyes flopping shut, super-glued, then at twelve, Dan smiled, pointed to the room and I slunk off like a collie who'd just dumped in his master's brogues.

But could I sleep? Those eyes! That look! The way he drank! The way he held his glass!

When would he come in? *How* would he come in? What was I going to do? Should I belt him? Or just jump out? But the bed was against the wall and I would be pinned on the wall side. Maybe I could vault over the top, or crash over the bottom somehow, or just vault over him and give him a not-on-your-bluddy-well-life-mate kind of a boot.

But it's all very well if by nature you are aggressive, if aggression comes easily to you. If it doesn't, the very thought drains you.

I lay weak as a child watching the door, thinking of Dan, crouched out there in the darkness, slitty-eyed and slugging țuica. I had visions, heinous visions of what was passing through his mind.

At about two I realised the whole thing was a joke and he was all snuck up with his Mrs so I closed my eyes, fell asleep and suddenly he was in the room. Whether it was an hour later or a minute later, I just don't know.

I gripped the sheet, all confused and three-parts asleep like a man fighting drunkenness, and God knows why I gripped the sheet, but I gripped the sheet. Baffled, lead-booted and struggling to get out I remember having battling thoughts of him creeping towards me with his trousers down.

I felt him catch hold of the sheets, pull them back and slide into bed. My heart was pounding and my mouth had gone dry. Was this real? A nightmare? Was I dreaming? When was I going to wake up? Should I belt him? Jump out? What? What?

'*Buna nopte,*' he said, turned on his side and slept like a child all night.

And I lay awake, sweating, boiled, waiting for the big roll over, the bid clutch, and for the long dark hours of that night gazed into the blackness of the ceiling, tensing at his every move. I felt like a demon next morning when he tumbled out of bed, fresh as day.

'*Buna dimeanața!*' he sang out, hurriedly dressed, went out, returned, handed me a nice big tumbler of lukewarm țuica, and smiled.

He was a really friendly guy, Dan.

Horse Talk

In the shadow of a wall down a cobbled backstreet in Appoldo de Jos, half a dozen octogenarians watched as I tacked up the horses. Among them was a venerable old chap with long white hair and a big moustache. He was dressed in a faded mauve Russian tunic and was squatting on a step by a door. He must have been a hundred. Beside him was an old biddy, all bent from a lifetime's work, big handed and dressed in black. What was the world coming to? they nudged one another – weren't foreigners supposed to be rich? look at this one – destitute! so poor he's had to come on holiday on horses! look at his clothes! and he couldn't afford a hotel! Poor man! Poor, poor man!

The old biddy came crabbing toward me and squeezed an apple into my palm curling my fingers round it with her big hands and a 'It'll be alright, my son' look in her pitying eye; 'It'll be alright!' The white haired man nodded. 'Yes, it'll be alright.'

Thing is, they weren't far wrong. I was getting a bit short and still had four countries to go. I counted my money earlier; it didn't take long. I had sixty lei – which, exchanging at a hundred to the dollar didn't add up to a lot – and 1,000 dollars. It looked like I was going to run out somewhere along the line, and goodness knows what would happen then.

But what do you do? You can't just throw it in, chuck the horses away and get a bus home, can you? So you get up on your pony and push off along the cobbles eating your apple.

'*La revedere!*' Dan shouted, waving away.

'*Sa traiţ!*' the old man wailed as we clattered round the corner and were gone to them.

I thought about that old man as we went along and reckoned he was probably an old dragoon: that's what he was: that was a cavalry moustache: pity he never came to talk. You see these old boys in Romania and they're always quiet. It's the ones who don't know anything, haven't done anything, like the little fellow with the big voice and new hat, those are the ones who come and bore you. I wonder why you always wind up with the ones who don't know anything but always talk the most? I wonder. It's the same everywhere, isn't it.

Anyway, we continued along this stretch of dirt track for what seemed like years, a day here, a night there, the horses going along nice and steady, then followed a compass bearing straight over a big hill to short cut to Alba Julia, and that was a lonely ride.

It took us through a great straggling village, right up onto a huge bowl of land, like the Aberdares. When we came over the brow the distance in front whipped your breath away. It stretched off and off and off, and made you feel tiny. So there was old Karo puffing away looking right out over this great fawn-coloured sweep and Puşa staring into the horizon, and we went out across that grass and I could see us from the sky, little blips of black in all that khaki.

It was silent, hot and windswept and took us hours to cross. We went down a steep bank on the far side, down to a big lake where two shepherd girls were washing pans in the water. We went right up beside them and Karo and Puşa drank the water and the girls watched us, just kneeling there by the water washing those pans. Then we left and made for the next range.

I imagined a conversation:

KARO: Where are we going? All this slogging on and on, but where? *Where?*

PUŞA: Dunno.

KARO: I mean, look at this place! It's the emptiest place on earth!

PUŞA: Fishface's gone and got us lost.

KARO: I seem to have been walking for ever! Where are we going? *Where? Where? Why?*

Down below us, white and glittering, with the river winding through, was Alba Julia, White Julia, an old Hapsburg fortified town.

And maybe this is a cliché, and I don't care, I like clichés, everybody uses them when they talk and nothing is quite as powerful as a good old cliché (who has ever improved on the poverty of church mice?) but that ride went on for ever and ever and bloody ever, amen.

We slung our hook by the river and went for a swim, and the water was good clear water, except for the oil. A group of picnickers picked us up and found us a night's billet in an old house where the owner had died a few weeks before. It was a creepy place filmed in dust. When I saw all this black on the windowsills I thought it was levelled currants half an inch thick, but it was dead flies, millions of them. I wondered if the old codger had snuffed it in there and no one knew and that's what all the flies were. The lights didn't work either and it all stank of rot. I was too bushed to care and slept on his bed while the horses grazed in the garden beneath a moulting plum tree. Karo cracked stones half the night and heralded the midnight moon in gaseous baritone.

The town Alba Julia is pretty fine, with big city walls and above one of the gates is a cell where they walled up three partisans during the rebellion against the Hapsburgs. They kept them there for a year before they dragged them to a cart and had their arms and legs broken. They had a way of convincing people they meant business in those days.

There's a big statue of Michael the Brave who united Romania in the 1880s (that might be wrong too, the chap spoke very fast and had a harelip). In the middle of town is a moated wall, on top of which runs a big nasty concrete rampart with barbed wire.

'What's that?'

'Hospital.'

'Hospital?!'

'Hospital for crazy people ... you know, political people, not so crazy ...'

A gulag: bang in the middle of town.

'Are there people in there?'

'Yes: some.'

And I got to thinking I'd never have liked to have crossed Romania in any other way than on a horse. The ways we found, the paths and tracks we followed and the unexpected places we wound up in. The hills we scrambled up and slid down, the wild and empty country we passed through, the poverty of people right up in the mountains with no roads to their homes, living in minute houses with beaten earth floors – you couldn't have seen any of this except from the back of a horse. It was all so rich. No other form of travelling can begin to be as rewarding. If you go by train or car, the world rushes past you, and you don't even get to smell it. All you get is somebody else's fag, or someone's B.O. Even if you're on a bike many of the places you can get to with a horse are inaccessible to you, and if you walk, they're too far.

But if you travel on a horse you go to these places, and feel the world as you move through it, every step, every scent, every breeze, every dimple in the ground, every beetle that scurries beneath hooves, it's always fresh. I'd sooner go with a horse because the horse drives you into village life: he's a point of reference, something to focus on.

Besides, it's good being with horses.

And I don't travel with them to be eccentric, or for a stunt, it's because of these reasons I have given, that's all. It's hard too, and there were plenty of times when I wanted to chuck it all in, go home, sit in front of a fire and read, or be with Chumpie or go down to The Crown, have Jeff Aldridge pull a pint and drink it with Jock Beesley and John Morris: watch old Keith playing dominoes and hear Stan Wheeler singing.

Plenty of times.

I wanted to go home the day I left Alba Julia. I wanted to be in The Crown that day because it was my birthday. Three years before, I spent my birthday sitting on the Yugoslavian border with Maria, a Greek horse. And now, this year, in Romania with two other horses, and a bad leg. Two bad legs.

Instead we went out of Alba Julia on a compass bearing of 270 degrees. There wasn't any road, no track, nothing. We just went through these magnificent little hills, saw no one, heard birds all day: there were no jets, no planes, no cars: nothing. It was a wonderful day. We went through Zlatina and followed a serpentine of a road pitching up in Almaşu Mare where, incredibly, in the only shop in this remote village, I found and bought two bottles of champagne and shared them with my horses. If there's any spot, any enchanted place I know, anywhere I'd want to go back to celebrate a birthday like that again, then it is near Almaşu Mare in central Transylvania – all those strange little hills, those valleys and streams.

I fell asleep beneath some willows by a brook in the afternoon, then rode through tall stacks of drying lucerne standing like regiments of mummies. In little cornfields men and women hand-scythed wheat, tied it in bundles, and stooked it in the evening sun.

We stayed the night in Vaţa then in the morning tried to find the road to Gurahonţ and failed. We were caught in rain, and we were deep in woodland.

And something happened in that forest that night when we were homeless and soaked, but I'll tell you later: about what happened when we stood heads together in the rain, all night in that lonely forest in Transylvania.

Ursa

We came out of the forest round about midday and passed through Gurahonț, where I bought a warm frothing jam jar of beer. Someone bought me another and another while the horses grazed barley grass outside. There were a lot of guys hanging round that place and though they were interested in the horses, they were more interested in the beer.

I left my chaps hanging up on the bar door in Gurahonț.

I don't know why I left my chaps hanging up on the bar door in Gurahonț. Maybe there was something about Gurahonț which destroys your memory? Maybe my chaps are still hanging up on the bar door in Gurahonț? Maybe I ought to go back and get them?

Anyway, I left my chaps hanging up on the bar door in Gurahonț, packed up the horses, got on Karo and we weaved along all over the road to Joia Mare that afternoon, where we spent a night with a family of Laurence Olivier look-alikes, and 1 don't know if Laurence Olivier had bad breath, but they did. Mrs Death-Breath was the worst. I reckon her breath was flammable. It kind of frizzed your hair every time she spoke to you. Sitting down to eat with them all was an experience: if anybody had lit a match in there I reckon we'd have all gone up – but that's because grandad Death-Breath had another kind of problem and he wasn't too shy about letting you know.

I'd come across death-breath before: Punch suffers from it; so does Mark Alderson's bull-terrier, Bill. I didn't see any bull-terriers in Romania, but these people had the same kind of problem. It seems to me to be something to do with toothbrushes. Toothbrushes are not plentiful in Romania and toothpaste is ungettable so *lots* of people have bull-terrier problems. Also it was while I was sitting down with the Death-Breaths I remembered about my chaps. I tell you, if you ever go to Gurahonț, watch their beer, and if you see anyone wearing a pair of faded lovat green chaps, they're mine.

Despite that, the interesting thing about the Laurence Olivier look-alike Death-Breath family was they were one brother short: he'd gone

125

– done the bunk. He was the youngest. Straight after the revolution he'd applied for and got a passport and vanished – next day.

I was staying in his room and picked up a book called *Limba Engleza*, an English language textbook. It flopped open at a page and the first thing I read was 'I want to be a worker in a toy factory.' He'd crossed it out with a heavy pencil line.

Wherever he is, I wish him luck.

I was aiming for Varşand, to cross into Hungary at the Giula crossing but I had no Coggins test for Puşa. We went to Ineu to get one.

When we got there it looked like the wrong place for that kind of thing and we walked straight through town, when in the last hundred yards or so a man jumped up from a bench and ran over to us. He twigged fast and ten minutes later the horses were stabled with the fire brigade across the street. The firemen who took them away were slightly gone and I got to share a few swigs of the local firewater they'd been going on, washed down with *apa de la sulph*', which, if you like that sort of stuff, is supposed to do you good. I thought it was foul: sulphur water.

All the time my horses were there, everyone called the fire station 'Hotel Pentru Cai'. Hotel for Horses. I wonder if it stuck? It rather suited it.

Gheorghe Csoncsik and his pretty wife, Florika, put me up for five days while new papers were being prepared. It's all very simple, particularly if your host knows the local vet, is friends with the brigade boss, and enjoys sampling the firewater as much as any of them. He liked *apa de la sulph*' too, but couldn't get me on it.

Gheorghe was a Hungarian/Romanian and spoke both languages. His family were Hungarian from way back. He didn't look Romanian, if there is such a thing, having a kind of smooth rather wise face, with salt and pepper hair.

I asked Gheorghe what the huge rambling fort was on the Crişul Alb.

'Professional school,' he replied. I didn't understand this. I did when we visited it. It was another grim place for mentally handicapped children. I didn't see any green Ladas there.

Gheorghe gave me a few words in Magyar: horse, *lø*; water, *vis*; barley, *arpa*; oats, *zop*; thank you, *köszönom*; hello, *szervusz*; goodbye, *viszontlátásra*; just a handful to get going.

He took me downtown too, introducing me to a few of his mates, and as we walked behind a girl, he said 'Ahh! Look at her! She walks like a goat!'

Eating arrangements with Gheorghe were varied, breakfast being produced sometimes, and sometimes not.

This day: no breakfast.

We went into Ineu instead to get some medicament for his mum's pig. Everything was shut.

'*Tot inchis!*' he shouted throwing his arms about, then saw the restaurant was open.

'Aha!' he said, surprised, happily. '*Una bira?*'

In we went. The place was heaving. Gheorghe must have had some kind of grip over the lad in charge because we were shown into the big room out the back. It was one of those windowless places they seem to reserve in restaurants all over the world specially to rip you off, calling them executive suites or some such ridiculous name, and they are always airless.

We sat down. The boy disappeared, returning a minute later with a bottle of vodka and some '*mich*'. '*Mich*' is a sort of kufta kebab, and it's dished up with a heap of mustard. It's not bad; it's very good when you're a bit peckish first thing in the morning and someone else is helping you to a tumbler of vodka. Then the beer came in. Beer after eating is always a bit of a struggle, especially after vodka.

We polished all that lot off and stumbled away to the vet to get the porker panacea. The vet was in. And not only did we get the pig medicine but also got the Coggins tests for the horses and both had passed.

That was cause for celebration.

We were both pretty lit up anyway, so we didn't take much persuading, and since the porker dope had to be administered straight away to the ailing porker at Gheorghe's mum's place, we went there. And there we got lunch – earlyish.

Well, I was still pretty bunged full of *mich* and beer and vodka, and not at all hungry, and didn't want to eat ever again. So was Gheorghe. It wasn't really food we were after, but his mother pressed us into chairs, poured out beer, which was nice, and țuica, which was sort of nice, then dished up soup and we pigged at her table, with soup, then potato and pickled peppers, a lot of thick bread and more beer and more țuica, and then more soup.

When all this had been cleared away, both of us sank back into our chairs unable to speak, or breathe, or move, when his dad brought in the wine and the main course, a great fish about the size of a gumboot.

'*Puftim!*' they said. 'Dig in!'

When we got back home to Gheorghe's place, Florika was cooking supper. Gheorghe rummaged about in a cupboard on his hands and knees for some more țuica when in came a friend. He was a mild-mannered man, moustached and heavily built: he must have been about thirty-eight. He poured out the țuica and we chatted, but he was quiet. He was wearing uniform and had epaulette flashes I'd not seen before. I asked what they were. He looked away. Gheorghe explained.

'Timişoara. The first in the army to turn against the securitate in Timişoara were given these.'

His name was Ursa.

In the hours that followed I listened to this gentle man tell his story.

In Timişoara, right at the beginning of the revolution, the army were lined up with their guns aimed at the belly of the crowd. The securitate positioned themselves in buildings around, with the best line of fire at the mob. The army was ordered came to fire. Ursa, and others like him, had family in the crowd. They hesitated. Surely the order was wrong?

Gunshots rang out. They came from the securitate.

The switch was sudden: the army had refused to fire and stood with their people. (I wish you could hear Ursa sing '*Eu Senten Roman*'. This is a great patriotic song.)

By the end of the day Ursa was bandoliered and machine gunning. The army pinned the securitate into various parts of the town, and Ursa had his hands full against a battery of fire coming from a church. It was wild, he said, crazy firing. Those in the church shot at anything that moved, women, dogs, cars – anything. The fire was intense.

At dawn next morning Ursa machine-gunned his way to the

church, blasted and booted the doors open, then sprayed the inside with gunfire. The resistance quickly died away, and finally stopped.

They counted thirty dead.

The oldest was fifteen, the youngest was seven: a group of children.

That story had taken him four hours to tell.

It wasn't easy for him. Sweat ran down his face. Tears filled his eyes. He picked at his fingers.

I think Ursa's a great man.

In a way, maybe he exemplified much of what I felt for Romanians, I don't know, he was a sort of touchstone, made sense of the whole place for me, and him and Gheorghe and Florika were all so uncomplicated, good to be with. Like Sandu or Gheorghe Martinescu, I found something brave and admirable in all of them.

And just as in Bābāiţa I was sorry to leave Ineu. I made good friends in Ineu. I just remember going down the road over the railway crossing and waving and it all felt so empty because I'd left nothing with them except horseshit – and whisky and a few packs of Kent – like I said, horseshit.

The way to Varşand was sixty, seventy kilometres and we did it in a day. We went straight up the Crişul Alb all the way, right to the border; tricky riding in some places, but on the whole it was pretty easy. Also, a beautiful, winding ride. If you do it, watch out for the big wooden bridge outside Chisineu Criş, about five or six kilometres on: there's a couple of boards missing in the middle: Karo managed it. And you'll hit the plain again too, and I'm telling you now, that one is vast. It goes all the way to Eger, in northern Hungary.

They call it the *putsza*.

As in Bulgaria, I was sad to leave. Romania is beautiful. Staggeringly beautiful, much of it locked in a past, places that have not changed for centuries. In some of those Transylvanian villages was a silence so deep, so profound it moved me to the quick. Sometimes, I even wondered if I had, like the children of the Pied Piper story, been transported to another a long gone past. It is, after all, the legend that the lost children ended up in Transylvania. Church bells pealed out of sight, the land rang with birdsong and the shrill of cicadas. The plains were empty save for some distant figure sailing by with horse and cart. Water buffaloes grazed in mirage. The buildings were peeling and elegant, the trees tall, still and dignified, the rivers and streams silver. The people smiling and strong.

In amongst all this, on some leg of this journey Karo, adopted a song. This is a strange thing for a horse to do, it might seem, but he did it anyway. From the day I first bought him, he'd been a vociferous kind of horse and made plenty of little noises, squeaks and grunts and groans. These now he put to effect and with each step of his forefeet delivered a rhythmic note. It didn't vary, not much anyway and was not at all unpleasant to listen to. In fact, it was, if anything, soporific. It gave to our journey a kind of equine score, a harmonious thread, lines of unwritten natural music.

KARO: Nhnn...nhnn...nhnn...nhnn...nhnn...

I even found myself joining in. It had a headiness to it, a relaxing texture. A voice of content, of peace. A peace that absorbed the landscape and everything in it.

We hit the border at eight that night as the sun set in a wall of fire. A line of glinting cars from the control point stretched back maybe half a mile or so and we queue-jumped. Once again, I had no transit visa, no export licence, no import licences, no international transport certificate, no T2. I didn't even have a visa for myself, and my Romanian visa had expired. But I had Kent cigarettes and whisky.

The vet took my papers. I bit my lip. He disappeared into his hidey-hole. The customs man took my horse purchase papers, and my passport. An hour went by.

Then the vet came out and smiled and there was this great red stamp straight across the horses' passports: it read EXPORT LIBER.

Then the customs man came out and handed me my passport and wished me *No rok!* Good Luck.

'*La revedere!*' they shouted as we walked away.

When I got to the Hungarian control point I didn't have any cigarettes or any whisky. And I didn't have any forints nor an entry visa and bla bla bla.

We slept in no-man's-land that night, and cold it was too. There wasn't any food and nothing to drink. The horses did better than me and got stuck into a roadside verge of clover.

At four next morning a customs official handed me a cup of coffee, and entry visas, transit visas, vet certificates and we were in.

Saddles on, horses packed and exuding equine gases, we stepped into Hungary at sun-up.

KARO: Nhnn...nhnn...nhnn...nhnn...nhnn...

Hungary

I'd been keen to get into Hungary because everyone said it'd be easy going, with all sorts of things to buy: new clothes, for instance, socks and stuff; all of which was very thrilling. I'd been wearing the same outfit for three months, and you can go off kit in that time.

And although I had adored Romania, I was glad of the change too because if anyone said '*as cumperat*' again I think I'd have gone mad. And I'd just about had it with țuica, palyinka and pork fat and was fed up with being hassled for dollars the whole time. I reckoned in Hungary you'd get better fare, there'd be wine and vegetables. Of course, I didn't know anything about Hungary, about its currency, whether there was a black market or not, or whether I was going to get ripped off by the banks or what. I don't like changing money in banks in communist countries because they try to rip you off worse than the gypsies, and although I knew Hungary was no longer communist, there was no guarantee the banks wouldn't still try to rip you off. Besides, which bank ever gave anyone a decent deal? If there was a black market in England I'd use it because you get a much more realistic deal on the black market, even if it does drive the chancellors of the exchequers, or whoever they are, up the wall.

Another problem was that any negotiation for changing money would have to be done in Magyar and Magyar is a bit of an art. On top of this I didn't know where we were going to find our lodgings, how difficult that was going to be, or where the horse joints were – all the usual snags, which somehow seem bigger when you change countries because at first you can't cotton a thing anyone says.

Anyway, we wound up in this camping place which robbed me of 27 dollars not including dinner so I had to go and ferret about downtown to find some place to fettle in and guess what I got?

Pork fat and palyinka.

They call it salonata, which sounds as though it ought to be better than pork fat, but it isn't, it's still pork fat. And palyinka is still called palyinka, exactly the same as Romanian palyinka only fifty times the price.

I could have killed for cabbage, I could. Pork fat! Was I sick of pork fat! I tell you, that was a serious blow. But I was hungry and wolfed that lot, then went for a wander around town.

Guila is very pretty with yellow painted churches and a fort with this nice open feel about it, and the shops are full. So you say: look at all this! Where are all the rows of rotten jam? Where are all the dusty shelves? All these flashy cars! There are thousands! All these radios and cassettes in shops, and tons of food. Look at these porno mags! All that flesh! What's going on? Why's it so dull? And the women in the shops they want to sell you things, really want to, and you can buy postcards, and send them, make telephone calls and really lose your shirt, it's amazing. And in the camping place there are showers with taps and pipes with hot water so you could wash and dry your gear. I looked at clothes in town but they were a lethal price, so it was back to the army fatigues, faded red shirt, and soap. I don't know what it all felt like. Neither foreign nor home; it just felt like being in a place where you could get everything and so it lost interest compared with Romania. The comparison being when you find yourself in a country that has so many links to the past, history becomes alive before your eyes. Time, somehow, has stood still, and in that oblique embrace you too, become lost to the present. When we pulled out of the camping place next morning I didn't know what I thought of Hungary because there wasn't anything to think.

We followed the river Körös, (which had been the Crişul Alb in Romania) right out of Guila – it's only a cough and a spit from the camping place – and about three miles on, a little fat chap standing beside a caravan full of bottles yelled out 'Hoi! Director non-stop!' pointing at himself.

'Director non-stop!' he shouted again. 'Beer! Coffee! Vodka! Non-stop! Hoi! Director non-stop!'

He was quick to have spotted us on the riverbank, and as he beckoned we went over to him.

I got off, tethered the horses in a scratch of grazing and went up to his caravan. He produced a large thermos and plastic cup, and without asking, poured out a coffee, but he poured it like a chemist pours acid, sort of stingily, checking he didn't do too much, holding it up to the light, and he had this swagger somehow, and did a lot of winking, with this shifty my-I'm-an-important-sort-of-geezer air about him.

He handed me the cup as I'm certain they handed Socrates hemlock, with that kind of we-know-what-you're-doing look in their eye. As I took the cup, he took out a small leather bag pulling from it a hundred Deutschmark note. This he held in the air, admiring, gazing through and into it, like a seer into a crystal ball transfixed by the magic within, lost to its mysteries, then with a magnificent flourish drew it to his lips, and kissed it.

'Director non-stop!' he breathed. 'Director Deutschmark!'

I'd just found my man.

I yanked out a dollar.

He pulled a face.

Lost to the blue of the note in his hand, he held it again to the light, and once more kissed the Deutschmark. Then he sighed and put it in his pocket. He took my dollar as one might take a filled child's nappy, examining it with the same level of disgusted distance. He leaned into the door of his caravan, all the while holding my dollar out at arm's length and with a great bountiful gesture, drew out a bagful of forints.

'Director non-stop forints!' was the new conspiracy, and he checked over his shoulder to see no one was watching.

He winked. 'Director non-stop dollars – forints,' and put my used nappy in a place somewhere out of sight.

I brought out ten dollars, which lightened things.

After a lot of wringing of hands, and stories of hardship and anguish, sorrowful tales of abandonment as a child, of ailments and illnesses that afflicted him, the number of operations he'd had for the diseases he'd fallen victim to, the wives that had left him, aged parents he had to look after, with an expression of utter misery, the bleakness of a future he faced, he offered fifty forints to the dollar, which I refused.

As he offered, I countered, and as the argument rose in pitch and sums ascended he recorded all in a small notebook with great pangs as though it took the very life out of him.

The bank directors non-stop, he groaned, were all crooks: only Lasky was good. The businessmen directors non-stop were also all crooks, only Lasky knew the real value of money, what dollars were actually worth.

Was I sure I didn't have any Deutschmarks?

Finally, after three hours, six cups of coffee and six glasses of brandy, he condemned himself to pay me 900 forints for ten dollars and he nearly cried when he handed the money over.

The bill for the coffee and the brandy was two dollars.

After further argument I paid, with complaint, trying to exact from him all the anguish he'd exacted from me when the tables had been turned.

Lasky was amazing, and the thing about him was he was the only black market dealer I came across in Hungary. And, what was more amazing was that, with the cost of the coffee and brandy taken in, he gave me a lousier deal than the bank.

We moved apart swearing everlasting friendship. I would invite him to England, to America, Malaya, Spain, Africa – everywhere – told him he ought to apply for the post of minister of finance for Eastern Europe and he roared a tirade of farewells as we jogged away in the noonday sun, finding ourselves somewhere near Békés at nightfall, and none too comfortable.

KARO: What d'you think of this place then?
PUŞA: Full of rats.
KARO: Fishface's been running round all night throwing stones! D'you hear him?
PUŞA: He's keeping me awake.
KARO: And doesn't he stink! Phew! Rats and pigs! Why did he sleep with the pigs?
PUŞA: They're the only ones that'll have him.
KARO: What a place! Fishface sure knows how to pick 'em.
PUŞA: He surely does, like that place back there when I woke up all covered in plums.

KARO: And where's all the grub? Fishface told us there'd be plenty of grub! Where is it then? *Where? Where?*

Next day was a burning day and we followed the river toward Kondoros but every watercourse swung stubbornly south which shoved us back into swanning through thousands of acres of head-high maize, stifling and airless on dead straight dirt tracks which halted at the edges of concrete irrigation channels which drove us back to our original route, and we'd have to find another way.

PUŞA: Why don't we go along the road?

Huge linear irrigators, like things from 'The War of the Worlds' swam in the sky above our heads as we passed – or shot underneath – because Karo thought they were related to cranes and wound Puşa and me up so tight we all got involved in this wild linear-irrigator-tearing-away-from game with unbridled and headless enthusiasm which was wearying, to say the least.

Thus it was, with cash running out, ripped off by the only black marketeer in the land, bereft of sleep and pouring with sweat, exhausted by horses, constipated by pork fat, stinking of ratshit, aching from palyinka and my clothes in rags, I journeyed through southern Hungary.

Blind in a Flatland

Hungary, like all Eastern European countries, has a lot of collective farms, and these can run up to fifty thousand acres apiece. And because the land is state-owned there are no fences so you can ride mile upon mile without opening a gate. I rode through all of Eastern Europe and never even saw a gate, never mind opened one. Hungarian farms are more modernised than others in Eastern Europe, being equipped with John Deere tractors, linear irrigators, huge crawlers, new combines, big dairy units and all manner of modern machinery.

Apparently they have the largest per capita output of any agricultural nation in the world: at least so the fellow in Gyomendrőd reckoned.

We were in the *ló istalló*, (this being Hungarian for horse-house), where there were a few other *lós*, all pretty big Nonius horses – which is what Karo was supposed to be, according to the vet in Ruse. But if Karo was a Nonius, then he was a weird Nonius, or maybe other Noniuses are weird Noniuses and Karo was a straight one, but if Karo was a straight Nonius then all other Noniuses are weird.

The fellow in Gyomendrőd who claimed Hungary had the biggest per capita output on earth also fixed up for the horses to be shod, which happened to be next day, and well shod they were too. The fellow who put the shoes on those horses was called Zőltan Vosko and he knew what he was doing.

Those shoes lasted for quite a few kilometres after that, were taken off, and put on twice again: they were some hard stuff, although the bloke in Poland who refitted them dolloped a lump of weld on to the fronts and sides, he used mild steel so they wore dead even: he was pretty good. Funny shaped shoes they were, with a clip on the front, one clip to the side and six nails. If they were heavy, they supported the heels well and the man who shod the horses that day, him and the farrier in Poland were the only ones on that trip who shaped the shoe to fit the foot. Usually, they do it the other way round and that lames a horse quicker than anything. Zőltan charged me twenty quid for both horses.

I gave him pounds because it was either that or dollars or nothing, but it was the last of my pounds. And while I remember, talking about money for a minute, travellers cheques don't work in Eastern Europe, at least, not unless you like hanging around banks all day.

But I've a tip, just in case you need it, which is this. If you have travellers cheques and the bank is taking all day, what you do is make a big point of going outside and writing down the address of the bank, go back in, ask for the name of the cashier and the manager, make a big point of taking down any other details you can think of and you'll get your money in five minutes. Works a treat.

Enough of that kind of twaddle – changing money is so *boring*, and I *hate* banks: they always manage to foul up your day, don't they? I tell you, wherever you are, the best tip is to find a black marketeer, but make sure it isn't Lasky.

Anyway, we got away from that place and out into the heat again. What all this made me aware of was that this country had done with communism, slung it out, I was in a place where the market ruled, and you had to pay. I don't resent paying, it's fine; so long as it's not too much. Just it's tougher on the homeless horseman with declining assets, that's all – him and his four-footed friends go a bit shorter, that's all. Ah, but give him the free-booting, ţuica-slugging, barrel-chested brawling Romanian with his back-slapping welcome any day! And maybe he can be a sluggard to stay with but you never forget him. Besides, it's cheaper and a lot more fun that way.

So there we were strolling along the river bank in all this heat worrying about money when a grim thing happened.

Karo blinded Puşa.

I didn't realise it at first. Puşa was acting the clown and throwing herself round like a ragdoll and put her head down round Karo's belly and he smacked her one. He got her a real corker, what with these big new shoes, catching her just above the left eye. Didn't she yell! I've never heard a horse make the indignant noises she did, but they were just exactly the same tone as a human: she was seriously angry with Karo, kept trying to hack him and was the very devil to hang on to, and he was scared of her – plenty.

It was only in the evening when I tethered them up the way I always did, I noticed she was fumbling around and sticking closer to Karo than normal. When I walked up to her she was very wary of me and only when I touched her I realised she wasn't seeing me. Her left eye was all clouded over, like a dead animal and at first I thought she was dying. I thought she'd poisoned herself, had picked something up, been at hemlock. The other eye seemed okay but that was clouding too. I didn't sleep much that night because I was worried and we were right out in the middle of nowhere so there was no chance of a vet.

Next morning, Puşa was worse, and when we got going, I knew it was the kick and she was going blind. Three days later she'd lost very nearly all her vision and there wasn't a vet in the place who knew anything about optical nerves and whether it's possible for a horse to be blinded by a kick. I even rang England, but no one could say, not without looking at her. She was not obviously blind, because Puşa is a very intelligent horse and when caught out by something is too smart to play the fool. But that left eye got smaller and smaller until it was half its size and the right one was going too.

There was no question of selling her: it wouldn't even enter my head. We just had to go on in the hopes of finding a vet who'd know what it was, if it's possible for a horse to be permanently blinded like that. So we went on, Puşa travelling as pack-horse, while I rode Karo. I held her close to me and often we'd be going along with her nose right up on my knee, and I'd be holding her ear and in those moments, I got very close to that pony.

At night I took her her food and helped her with it and brought water to her and she was very good and gentle and didn't throw herself about. I bathed her eyes in cool water and she stood still so I talked to her, but she got blinder. And I'm sure Karo knew what he'd done because he was acting guiltily with her and at night would keep very close even though every now and then she'd really lambast him, like she was saying he was a rotten sod for blinding her.

For day on day we just went on like that, and no one had the first idea about what to do. I just carried on with the water and sponges and carried on riding Karo and holding Puşa's ear. We were following this canal going north and I was aiming for the Czechoslovakian border somewhere above Eger, but we were still well south. I thought maybe we ought to make for the place where the Hungarian cowboys were, Hortobagy, and so we went up the canal and wound up in a place called Örményes instead, and that was a good find.

There's a fellow in Örményes called Csaba Török, and he's a friend of mine now. His wife is called Elizabeth. She found some stuff for Puşa's eye, and some other stuff for my leg which was still swollen from the kick from the white mare. Elizabeth mended my clothes and fed me, while Csaba gave me a good time and they and a friend called Alexander Szava, they patched me and the horses up, and pushed into me an understanding of Hungary in the tangle of Eastern Europe.

Csaba spoke good English. He'd been to Gödöllő University where he majored in agriculture, and was an agricultural engineer: the agricultural engineers in Eastern Europe are always well educated, quite a slice above the average. Csaba had also spent eighteen months in America, having been sent there for work experience by the Ministry of Agriculture in Hungary and hosted by the International Farming Association.

He worked on various farms here and there and at the end of the eighteen months had a goodish wad of bucks put by but instead of misering it away, he got Elizabeth over. They bought a thundering great Chevy Impala, drove all over America and blew all the money on having a ball.

'Free as a bird ve voz!' he chuckled, lighting up. 'And it voz the right thing to do. Do you know what ve did vith the car? No? Ve got to Kennedy Airport, got out, slammed the door and valked avay! Ha! It voz a good car! The engine voz the size of a Trabant! It drank three gallons of petrol in one hundred kilometres! Yah, it voz an expensive bitch, but a good vun!'

Man after my own heart, Csaba.

As he talked he seemed to be lost in a memory and stared right off like he remembered it all clearly. I guess he did.

He had big blue eyes, Csaba, and a King Henry beard, and he had this catching laugh, like everything on earth was a hoot, and he couldn't see anything without finding something daft about it and he knew how to have a good time.

He went on to say when he got back from America he felt really down and was impatient for change. It was the beginning of his career and he wanted to move quickly; he'd been bitten by the American bug. The local communist leader at the time told him that if he wanted to get on, he had to join the communist party.

'But I don't think that vay,' he said.

'In that case, you will not get on,' he was told.

This was all back in 1986, four years before, and in September that year there was a meeting in Lakitalek of actors, writers, engineers, poets – anyone who wanted to speak out – irrespective of the wideness of the political profile. So the Democratic Forum was born. A letter was sent to all the newspapers, and people went round the towns preaching democracy. The system grew and slowly they broke the grip of the communists. The orthodox communist party was shattered completely. The socialist party pushed from the inside and the Democratic Forum from the outside. The elections in March 1990 saw the final end of communism, with six parties in parliament.

'Suddenly there were no communists!' Csaba exclaimed, throwing his arms out. 'It voz like a vind blew them all avay!'

He talked about the collectives and what to do about them, and reckoned that the way forward was simply to let the market decide, that is to say, not to destroy everything in the way the communists did after World War II, but to move with caution, with the market, and be sensitive to market conditions.

Then I met Alexander Szava. He was a big man, with presence and cool intelligent eyes. He'd been a party leader, but gradually grew to see through the system and was now overall boss of the collective at Örményes, a 5,000-acre estate.

Like Csaba, he was hopeful about the future, but talked about investment, not charity or palm-off hand-outs from Margaret Thatcher, of which there had just been one – a £5,000,000 management-training aid package, or some such chunk of governmental jargonise.

'That means our people go to England, get taught by English

professional management training types and the money stays in English pockets. We're not fooled,' he said, 'And we're not interested. We want business. Up-front business, put-your-money-where-your-mouth-is capital.

'Eastern Europe is ripe for investment, here particularly – but look at it historically for a moment.

'The problems of Eastern Europe are not ours alone. The Yalta Agreement after the Second World War, and the Entente Cordiale after the First just pitched a problem into our laps now. There's not a border in Eastern Europe that'll not be in dispute. Do you realise how much land was actually carved up? Do you understand the passions involved? Two sick old men washed their hands of us and gave us to Stalin, and what a knife he had. We lost Transylvania, the Dalmatian coast, the Bulgarians Macedonia, the Romanians Moldavia: in affected the Serbs, Slavs, Czechs and Slovaks – none of their borders today are real sovereign borders – not in terms of their people – there are families divided on either side. You know, we are afraid. What on earth can we do? Do we just say "our borders are inviolate and we shall not interfere with yours" when there are people on either side screaming to be Hungarian or Romanian or Bulgarian or Serb?'

Alexander sat back and waited for that to sink in. We were sitting in his holiday house on the banks of the river Tisza, a river not unlike the Po, but with deeper sides.

'And investment. We desperately need investment. We are hardworking intelligent people and have been misled for a long time. If the monster Russia imposed this on us, then surely it impinges on the raw decency of the West to dig us out of a hole you were responsible for sticking us in. I remember listening to tanks when I was very young, Russian tanks, five metres apart, day after day pouring into Budapest to stamp out the 1956 Revolution. We cried out for help then – but you had Suez, and we lost. And what have we got now? Again? Now it's Iraq. Will the West forget us again? We were absolutely crushed by Russian weight then. You know, that was terrifying. What I am saying is that we have thrown our doors open to you, and you've been pretty faint-hearted about taking advantage of it. Of course there's uncertainty, of course there are other kinds of problems that still have to be ironed out, but I thought your Thatcherite business-tycoons had balls. Or haven't they?

'Tell them to come over here! We can do business. And don't worry about the Russians, we know how they think – we've had forty years of practice.'

Stuck for an answer, he slapped my back. 'Have a brandy! *Egészégédre!* You know, we've got a lot to offer. You've seen our rivers, our horses, the wildlife here. You've been out in the sunrises and sunsets, you've seen our agriculture. We can look east for markets: Russia is starving: look at our position geographically: and East Germany – that's a virgin market. As each of these places begins to unravel they'll be looking for stuff to buy and we can supply. We might not have your experience in marketing, but we have determination, good land, good farmers and we are charged with all the vigour of novelty.'

I swallowed my brandy. There was little I could say.

Hitch-hiker Csabika

For me, the national park of the steppes of Hungary, Hortobagy was all a bit overdone. All that whip-cracking and icecream wrappers rolling through the dirt, the car parks and cafes, museums, market stores and tourist gimmicks, lost it for me. Everybody was trying too hard to make something of it, and really it's just a great grassland plain with horses and cowboys. Sure, it's the real *putsza*, and those are real cowboys in their blue cloaks and flat black hats, and those are nice horses, fancy big stables, and those are old creaky sweep wells and the heat screams across the plain as hot as any wind in Saudi, but it was just too self-conscious.

I was glad to return to Palyinka Palace in Örményes with Csaba.

But you can't land yourself on someone forever, so one morning I said I must go before I got kicked out, because Puşa's eyes were better.

Then along came a hitch-hiker. I was to have company. The company of Csabika, and he was going to ride Karo.

KARO
Nhnn...nhnn...nhnn...nhnn...nhnn...

I borrowed an old military saddle from Csaba and at eleven in the morning, a bit late for riding, I set out with Puşa, and Csabika with Karo and we rode up-river towards Fusesabony. We covered forty kilometres or so then fetched up in Abádzolók, a watery place with a big lake and sailing boats, drowning islands, speedboats and helicopters.

Apparently it compares with Lake Balaton in central Hungary but without the pizazz, so it's better. It's a pretty place actually. And there was a fellow there in the horse place who doesn't know what's outside his back door. He put us on a route and within a hundred yards he was wrong. I told you: people just don't know what lies at the bottom of their gardens, it's amazing. I expect I'm the same, although I like to think I know where all the springs and streams are at home, where you can see

144

newts or where the buzzards nest, where the streams run in the valleys and whether you can get through by horse, I like to think so.

Csabika was a great travelling companion, getting what we needed, organising drinks, where to stay, what to pay, where to eat and where to find water. And he didn't care about the dirt or the heat or the flies, but just kept on going, all the while humming or singing softly to himself, or maybe to Karo, saying *'igen, igen'* yes, yes, or *'nem, nem'* no, no, or *'jó, jó'* (pronounced yo, meaning good: you hear it all the time).

In one place we were stuck without water, so we went up to an old disused well and lowered my folding bucket down into it, with a stone in and the bucket lashed to a tether rope, and we drew up water. The water was pretty rank, but when you and your mate and your horses are thirsty, I mean really thirsty even if the water stinks, it's still water.

We called on a solitary house.

14 August 1990
I am now drinking rough white wine in a rough white house as hot dry winds burn across the withered grass out in the putsza. The fields are black, crops harvested, only sunflowers hang their heads in the sun and the chicory in all the fawn will remain a pale sapphire in my memory. A gate bangs on a hinge outside, a tractor engine runs. The windows are dirty, men are covered in sweat, grimy, wiping gritty arms over gritty faces. This is a hot place, a hot day. This is not pony weather. And that had been a long ride.

We went across country ignoring all the roads, just going along across fields of cut corn, and through woodland, following a route of 350 degrees north. We went up and down irrigation ditches, weaved through collective farm yards, crossing rivers and streams as we came to them and though the landscape was flat, some of those big ditches were not easy to cross.

When we got to Füsesabony we stayed there in the horse place on the side of the road, then in the morning made to get away from the town and got tied up in a massive railway junction and the only way out was back.

But Csabika fixed it. He signalled to me to go over to the station.

But there were all these cars, and railway lines with trains screaming past. No, no, I said, never. He nodded his head and said *'igen, igen, toonnel! toonnel!'* and so I went and there was this impossible pedestrian precinct right under the trains and it was full of people.

'No,' I said. 'Never.'

Csabika said yes, and I wound up holding the horses and down he went into that tunnel and he yelled at everybody to get out the way because there was an Englishman coming with a pair of horses and down we went. I can tell you it's no joke going through somewhere like Paddington underground at rush-hour with a pair of horses. Never do it. I don't know why no one got killed, I don't know why we made it.

He was amazing, Csabika.

And there were a few more things about Csabika. Though he rode a hundred kilometres with me, we spoke not a word of one another's language, and though he rode a hundred kilometres on Karo, it was the first time he'd sat on a horse.

And though he did all he did for me, all that organising, finding stables and places to stay, he did it as a boy.

Csabika was ten years old.

He was Csaba and Elizabeth's son.

I left Csabika, and Csaba and Elizabeth after they settled me with Ferenc Szamaguōlgyi and his wife Ildikó in Maklar. We caroused ourselves to death in the local gypsy bazaar listening to vibrant gypsy music, where everyone played everything from spoons to dustbin lids by way of violins. The music was raucous and rowdy, with plenty of life but the tavern owners were not keen for anyone to buy the gypsies a drink.

'Firewater,' he said. The gypsies all looked pretty well lit up to me anyway, and it'd been my experience that a jug of firewater makes them really rowdy – I couldn't see another flagon would have made any difference.

'Viszonlátásra!' Csaba called out of the car window. I leaned in to say goodbye and little Csabika was in tears.

He really liked Karo.

Karo's a very likeable horse.

And I liked Csabika.

KARO: I wish we could have stayed.
PUŞA: Me too. Grub was good.
KARO: And that little fellah – he didn't weigh a thing.
PUŞA: Unlike Fishface.
KARO: Now where're *we* going?
PUŞA: I dunno, I can't see a lot, can I?
KARO: Aren't those mountains?
PUŞA: Oh no! Not more mountains.

Of Crooks and Goblins

Ferenc Szamaguōlgyi was a keen horseman, and, like Csaba, was also an agricultural engineer. He knew about a horseplace in Eger so next day he rode Karo, accompanying me to the house of some friends, them the four of us rode on from there to Petro-Tanya, a Lipizzaner Stable, run by an ex-cavalry commander and driving champion Victor Matyus.

We rode through the foothills of the Bűkk mountains which are like soft folds in a great blanket thrown across the land. In those valleys were draughts of cool air, trees and streams and the colours were African.

The other two riders were a couple of friends of Feri's. One rode a Lipizzaner and the other a biggish bay and he rode her in western gear with a nylon saddle blanket. I don't know who's daft enough to make saddle blankets in nylon but they sweat up a horse and draw its back like sponges. Synthetic stuff isn't good next to skin.

I'd had a bad time with those rotten army ponchos and finally ditched mine after André brought out another from Janet Cross of Ridry in Devon. Hers not only kept the wet out but didn't sweat up either, it was a better shape and didn't spook the horses. It was cotton-based. I only like natural fibres and I'm sure the only kit that works on horses is cotton, leather, canvas, brass and steel. It's been my experience that all artificial materials will let you down right at the wrong moment, and the worst of the lot is nylon.

So there was this guy riding nicely enough on that young mare with her back all of a froth and when we arrived at Petro-Tanya, he left her out in the sun where she boiled, while he drank a few beers in the shade then rode her home.

I couldn't do it. Petro-Tanya is a stud and in the main stable are two lines of Lipizzaners. They're like a couple of lines of White Gods, all wreathed in togas and airs.

All over the walls are photographs of them performing in gleaming harness or being ridden by fantastically-clad horsemen in The Spanish Riding School.

My two hairy little crooks got shoved up round the back somewhere.

'Tsigani-ló!' they got called. Light-fingered horses. Gypsy horses.

They looked small and wicked, glinty-eyed and shifty: they were casing the joint.

'You've got to watch them,' I said to the man as he exchanged their headcollars for nylon ones. 'They're clever: they'll whip those things off, knock the rails down and get out.'

'No they won't,' he said.

Day ended, and we all went off to town, leaving the horses. We came back at midnight, and turned in. Everything was quiet.

KARO: Just one more tug – that's it! Where's the grub?
PUŞA: Pssst! Over here! Here!
KARO: Whehey!
PUŞA: ... munch, munch, munch ...
KARO: ... munch, munch, munch ...
PUŞA: Right! Scarper!

Next morning, the hairy crooks were in their places, nylon at their feet, rails on the ground.

The souls of innocence.

Missing: one bag of oats.

Rifled: one bag of barley.

Vanished: one stack of lucerne.

They had the gall to whinny for breakfast.

'Tonight we chain them,' the man said.

Petro-Tanya's a nice place. Go and stay with Victor Matyus. He knows everyone from Prince Philip down. He'll treat you to a drink.

'Eine kleine disinfectio!' he'll offer. Then another. And another. And he'll show you all his photographs of driving Lipizzaners, of grand cavalry parades, of horsemen and horses. He's interesting. Then when you've seen all the photographs, he'll give you another kleine disinfectio, then suggest one more – just for luck.

He didn't charge silly prices either. For me and my two horses for two nights was 5,000 forints, which, at Lasky's rate, was about 65 dollars. Maybe some western businessman would make more of it as a business, but it was still partly state owned, so maybe the incentive to make a lot of it wasn't quite there.

Staying at the same time as me was a German family by the name of Mallison. Anyone who speaks German the whole time you would imagine to be German, wouldn't you? So I was surprised when I twigged that Mrs Mallison was English. And not only was she English, but she was a vet. And not only was she a vet, but she was a horse vet. And not only was she a horse vet, but she vetted horses for endurance rides. And not only did she do that, but she vetted internationally.

Now wasn't that a funny thing?

She peered into Puşa's eyes.

'If I had my shuftiscope, I could tell you what the problem is, but I haven't. I didn't expect to be peering into horses' eyes on holiday.'

She gave Karo and Puşa a quick once-over and to have a really fine horse vet check the running tackle on your nags and give them the O.K. is marvellous. We'd been through quite a few vet checks one way and another but none of them had checked the horses out the way Juliette did. I took her address in Western Germany and copied it down very carefully.

'If you're passing through, drop in,' she said. 'We're probably on your route.'

I bet she really regrets that now.

Then she gave me a tube of ointment she just happened to be carrying round with her.

'It'll help her eye – it's pretty safe,' she said. 'I use it on everyone: horses, dogs, cats, children, Folker (her husband). Marvellous stuff.'

I used it on everyone too. Karo, Puşa, me ...

'Just watch that mare though,' she went on. 'She won't be able to judge distance properly: don't take too many chances down cliffs.'

I had company again to Silvasvárad: this time Ferenc's wife Ildikò, the chap with the nylon saddle rug and Lidice's son. We rode through the Bukk mountains and that's the best bit of Hungary I saw.

We got to Silvasvárad, which was where the World Carriage Driving Championships were held in 1984, and it's an uninspiring place. The Lipizzaner studs are there, the place is full of them, but there's nothing else. Not unless you like plastic toys and rubber rings and tack like that – God knows why anybody wants that stuff.

Then a Lipizzaner landau flashes past, the coachman's whip catches in the sun, the horses serious, blinkered, proud – what beautiful creatures they are. So you catch yourself admiring the coquetry of the whole thing, the sudden surprise, the grace of phaetons and the pawing greys in dappled shadow beneath moving trees, the elegance of the horses' heads bent at the poll. So you level your camera for the finest shot the world has ever seen just as this tourist lunges into frame and he's wearing a pair of pink stretchy nylon ball-crushers and his girlfriend, hanging round his neck in a wrestler's embrace, is similarly clad in pink stretchy nylon shorts only she's swallowed hers.

The horses got stabled with a line of Lipizzaners, my pair adding an air of Monty Python's Flying Circus to the gravity of it all.

'*Tsigani-ló!*', the gypsy horses, the Lipizzaners tender rightly called them – members of that dusky group of wanderers who slink about devilish and en famille, squint-eyed and full of mischief. Yes, he was right about them.

I noticed the feed bin in the Lipizzaner's house.

I warned their tender.

'Nem, nem,' he said, 'nem problem.'

Next morning, the goblins' headcollars were at their feet.

Missing: 20 kilograms of oats.

The goblins whinnied for their breakfast.

'Tsigani-ló!' the tender cried, throwing his hands up.

I discovered Puşa's stash. She was furious. I added two more apples to it, which quietened her. She's the only horse I have ever known to deliberately hoard food. Karo fixed his eyes on it. The Lipizzaners shuffled from foot to foot. What will the gypsies do? Will the dusky wanderers kick hell out of one another? A family tiff? Will they fight over the prize? Or, will they once again under cover of darkness steal their way to the cornbin? Eat the Giants' breakfast? The Giants looked worried.

While the man in the heavy horse department tried to resolve the difficulties of how to contain my two varmints, I scuttled off to a local restaurant.

The food I had was good, the menu written in Magyar and German, then the bill came. It arrived in the form of a waiter with a notepad and wallet and he then asks what you had. If you've tucked into the wine a bit, it's a job to remember, particularly if you didn't know what you were ordering in the first place. So what you get and what you pay for is apt to be random. I paid about 500 forints for that one which was about five quid, which wasn't bad.

22 August 1990

It was three years ago today I set out from Assisi with Gonzo. We left at seven or so in the morning on 270 degrees going north under the Basilica Superiore and I remember how the bell tolled just as the town disappeared from sight. I remember the boom of the bell and how it felt like good luck, and how gentle the countryside was. It's the same here. We set out this morning on 350 degrees north into soft country weaving our way through the fields away from Silvasvárad. It was not hot: overcast with BBC 'sunny intervals'. The vine-growing region we left behind in Eger with its caves and grottos. Here the landscape is wilder, cultivated in part, the villages, like Italian villages, sleepy in the sun. They're prettier than others I've seen in Hungary, the houses older, painted yellow for the greater part, somehow reminiscent of Romania, with decorated lintels and jambs. It's a pity new houses are so plain.

We spent the night in Kirald in a great Stalinesque building. It left us fifteen kilometres to the border, an easy step and when we got there we were turned back – no visa.

A Train Journey

We were saved by a man called Jòsef Klobusovski. I don't know why he saved us. There we were hanging about like the thirteenth lost tribe in the middle of Bànrève not knowing what to do next, having just been slung out of Czechoslovakia because I didn't have a visa. Jòsef came via the *public bar* grapevine. I found it alwys worked: when in schtuk, go to the *bufe* and they give you a drink, someone will fathom out what the problem is and then everybody shins about like pigs after acorns and usually, usually you get sorted.

Josef had to move half a ton of scrap iron from his stable before my crooks were allowed in. He got kicked for his pains. He didn't complain. Clutching his knee we struck up this agreement in which I'd go to Budapest to get my visa and he'd look after the horses. He saved us, but why? Specially after that boot!

So I got on the train.

And as for the train journey to Budapest – I can see no reason on earth for wanting to travel anywhere on a train. First of all there's the business of the ticket, which in a foreign country is always an incomprehensible fiddle and you always wind up with the wrong sort. Then you have to hang round in some gloomy station where there's nowhere to sit. And if you ask someone if your ticket is for such and such a train, it involves the entire platform so you're left more confused than you were before. And there are never any bogs. Nor *bufes*.

When the train finally arrives, it's late, and you have to climb on behind a fellow who's carrying a set of chimney brushes and in front of some old woman with an armful of poultry or fence posts or something, so you're prodded and pecked between these two and have to fight your way down some impossible corridor arriving in a carriage which is either freezing because the windows won't shut or boiling because they won't open. In either event, the fellow who sits next to you smokes compost the whole way and heaves his heart out every five seconds while his Mrs struggles to control a herd of bawling children who are all regurgitating half-digested chocolate on one another. If there are bogs on the train they won't work or they're so heinous they're past trying – I remember being caught like this once in the meseta in Spain. I'd been sharing watermelons and wine from a gourd with some gypsies when the train suddenly ground to a halt. Outside it was roaring sunshine. We, the occupants, smothering within were all suddenly seized with Montezuma's revenge and there was no bog. Dare we risk shinning off the train? Make a dash for it to the nearest visible bush fighting trousers and belts, clutching that precious piece of paper, praying hard for the train to remain? Or sit tight

Six of us made for the bush.

The ensuing scramble on to the departing train with half-masted trousers, outstretched hands, the floundering footsteps struggling to avoid the turning wheels proved the wrongness of our decision. Then the other thing about trains is the noise. You can't hear yourself think. Hour upon hour of mind-crushing clattering, while over your head in the rack something totters around threateningly, and dribbles a line of tomato puree into your hair and what's his name opposite falls asleep his mouth open, also dribbling, head banging from side to side as he tries to cat-nap on seats made of pebbles roughly covered in flea-infested plastic.

Behind rusting wagons of ballast from steel mills the countryside flashes past. But you can't see it properly because the windows are filthed-up and when you arrive at your destination, it's always in the back-end of town, where accumulated to greet you are all the pick-pockets, drunks, bandits and whores the place can dredge up. Finally, if you can find one, the taxi driver rips you off.

I was very glad to be back in Bànrève to step off a nightmare and sit down with my saviour, Jòsef.

I suppose I should say something about Budapest, but I don't see how because I was only there as long as it takes to get a visa because I can't stand cities however grand or wonderful they're supposed to be and yes, Budapest was very nice but a serious rip-off.

I was lucky. I was whisked about in a green Range Rover, courtesy of the Military Attaché – or rather acting Military Attaché Wing

In Transylvania

After a ţuica breakfast

A drink at a sweep-well

Oxen, Transylvania

Transylvania: horse-drawn, unmade roads – a step back into another century

Families in Colun

Above: Ursa, who told me the story of the day the army stood with the crowd against the securitate.

Left: Sorting out the paperwork for exporting the horses from Romania to Hungary. It took several bottles.

Opposite: Village craft in Zlatna

Jòsef's grand-daughter

Above left: Gavin's soup. *Above right:* Gavin and the horses in front of a church in Czechoslovakia

Sir Karo with Gavin

Gavin is a shepherd at heart

Right: Karo rolling in long grass after a hard day of trekking

Below: Puşa after a few thousand kilometers, with Juliette Mallison

Commander Gaynor who'd just been given a MiG21. I wondered how Zog was doing with the T34.

Jim Bowden, another Military Attaché, supplied me with another one of Bob Gordon's get-you-out-of-trouble letters. Peter, the driver, zipped me over to the Czech Embassy and within the hour, I was back on the clattering hell, bound for Bànrève, so all I can say about Budapest is I've been there.

25 August 1990
Up at seven, which was a lie-in, feeling bloated. Breakfast was at eight with huge sausage which I had urged upon me by my smiling hosts. We understand not a word of one another's language. Magyar has eluded me completely. Following breakfast I took some children for pony rides, exercised the horses round Bànrève which is not a pretty place though I'll say it has heart. Also very peaceful. Then, afterwards, with nothing to do, I cleaned Jòsefs harness since he has two draught horses, both very good. It was a lovely bright morning and I don't mind cleaning tack in sunshine. Old Jòsef sharpened scythes opposite and kept blowing me kisses. The hours trickled past. Then it was lunchtime.
For lunch we had the same as supper, only hotter. Offered chicken in a kind of casserole, I wolfed it. I always wolf food. Consequently I am given more. Wolfing is taken for hunger. In my case it's not: it's the opposite. So I got rather a lot more. On the table was a pile of jam which I took to be a sort of cranberry sauce which I applied to my chicken only to discover I'd eaten my pudding with my main course, much to everyone's delight.
By one o'clock I was unable to move. At two I was handed a bicycle and Jòsef and I pedalled over to his daughter's place an indigestion away where we were given cakes and wine, and when we got back to his place at four, everyone was grilling up pork fat.
However, it was during my visit to Jòsefs daughter I learned with interest that like the Romanians, most of these people have built or have had a hand in building their own houses. Communism

has bred them this way and they're all good with their hands. They work for a pittance at some brutally inhuman job in a factory somewhere, then with black economy and time sparing they carve out another livelihood altogether since during the building of their house they will have hit on something they're good at and so you get villages full of people all with varied talents and skills and they put them to good use.

But to continue. The pork fat was confusing since, being accustomed to barbecues and bris I was thrown completely when handed a chunk of fat and slice of bread. The trick, I discovered, was to hold the fat in the flames until it dissolved then drool it over your lump of bread, like dripping. Trying my best to have my fat consumed in the flames I was corrected and got an even bigger bit and what with the red wine, raw onions, hot sun, smell of pigs, I wondered who would be the first to the lavatory.

By eight I was done for.

All was finished, the handful of pig-eaters departed and for supper we had duck, one each, followed by more jam and a kind of roly-poly pudding which gave me rigor mortis.

The parting goodnight shot was that for breakfast we should have all the pork fat we didn't eat for supper and the remaining two ducks.

Tomorrow I leave for Czechoslovakia. Tonight I was invited to:
1. Drop in on another Jòsef at eight o'clock tomorrow morning for a quick palyinka on my way to the frontier.
2. To drop in on the bar just down the street for a bit after I'd seen Jòsef and had a drink with him.
3. To call in on the bistro up at the border point to have one last vodka with the vet.

We had cold duck for breakfast and pork fat.
Then Estike, Jòsef's wife made me up a packed lunch of duck and pork fat and tomatoes, and a couple of bottles of beer, and I had a drink with Jòsef, and dropped in on the bar, and had some vodka, quite a lot of vodka with the vet, and then got to the

border three hours later – it's only one kilometre from Jòsef's place – did all the paperwork and now I'm in Czechoslovakia, half-drunk, it's boiling hot, I reckon to be constipated for a fortnight and night is falling. The horses are equally gorged.

He was wonderful, Jòsef Klobusovski and his wife Estike, and we all parted with wet eyes. But what warmed me so much to Jòsef was that he was without doubt the finest horseman I'd met in Eastern Europe. Karo and Puşa were turned out as they had never been turned out and he would have it that he did it. They'd had the best stables they'd been in, had their hooves oiled, and were groomed constantly, then wiped and groomed again. And for his industry he would accept nothing: and for his industry he received another booting from Puşa. He didn't complain.

Jòsef was definitely one of my favourites.

The Last Fart of the Ferret

Have you ever slept in a freshly peed-in bed: peed-in by somebody else, that is? No?

I have.

It happened like this. We – Karo, Puşa and I – had been in Czechoslovakia a few hours. We had a lunchtime graze on a river bank somewhere. I polished off the rest of the duck and the beer and pork fat, then slept in the sun and woke up bunged-up – you know, like I'd just eaten six pounds of Evostik. I felt awful and looked forward to a night's kip.

Since night was falling and we had nowhere to stay we made for the nearest village to ask for a kon-dom. I imagined the language to be Slav.

Well, it is and it isn't. No one knew what I was talking about so once again, off to a flying start I had by way of gesture and signs to make out we were after a night's lodging somewhere and all of that turned into a protracted three-hour negotiation with me waving my arms about and everyone else looking on as if trying to guess what the charade was and win a bottle of sherry, and then it would be their turn.

Fortunately, or unfortunately, the people who were my assistants in this instructive pastime were a gang of gypsies who found it all to their taste and nicely amusing and so we all played it and no one knew what was going on until someone finally twigged I was looking for a stable for the night and then I was hurried along with the horses to this decrepit but formerly dignified house with a large stable at the back, a barnful of lucerne and a bog of horrendous instability.

'Perfect!' I said. Everybody was delighted and out came the palyinka.

No one, however, reckoned on where I intended to sleep until one chap, a little more thinking than the others, slipped off and reappeared a few minutes later with a diminutive little woman who was as broad as she was tall, gold toothed, stockily limbed, wearing an apron covered in blood of some newly butchered chicken, or pig or something.

Anyway, I wasn't certain whether I was supposed to get involved with this dear lady for the night or what, so sat tight, hoping she wouldn't be forced on me, or me on her and sort of nodded as if to say, yes very good, like some half-cut cat judge at a dog show. After about ten minutes she turned on her heel and stomped off bitching at the top of her voice and by this time darkness had fallen, so I got my fleabag out and made towards the stable to spend the night with the horses.

'Nem! nem!' my hosts cried, which was Magyar.

Then one of them took me by the arm, led me inside the house which was lit by a single unshaded dust-covered bulb, hoicked a small sleeping child out of bed and with a grand gesture offered me the bed, then smiling, closed the door and left me in darkness.

That child had just pissed that bed. About ten seconds before.

And no matter how you try to avoid it, fresh pee stinks, and as the night wears on it stinks more and by morning you're choking, the room has become unbearable and you exit retching at dawn and when you visit the horses, even they back away from you and the worst of the lot was that my hosts thought it was me who'd done it.

I had a chance to look at the place in the morning when no one was around before I'd been blamed for pissing their bed and it was every bit as squalid as the gypsy places in Bulgaria and Romania. By this time I was looking more like a gypsy than the gypsies with my trousers once again falling to pieces, jacket torn, and now smelling of pee and short of money, I could pass fairly convincingly as a gypsy and was taken for one as I left the village – under a cloud which was none of my making, at seven – after having given the child-piddler pony rides up and down Pavlovce and the both of us stank to high heaven.

So it was at lunchtime I arrived in Rimavska Sabota collective angling for another hole-up in order to get to a hotel because I couldn't bear myself any longer.

The first man I asked at the collective about staying made it pretty clear that perestroika hadn't reached Rimavska Sabota and I'd better be on my way. The next fellow was absolutely plastered and was looking for a drinking companion while the third was a marvellous fellow and, though he talked to me from an ever increasing distance, got me booked into the collective and was then seconded into driving me with his car window open to the Hotelovy Preukaz in town, which had a room, though they were loathe to let it. Not until I showed dollars did they finally give in and I was allocated a room away from other guests. The room cost thirteen dollars per night, or 345 krona.

The view from my bedroom window showed a typical communist town with ugly, squat concrete buildings in the foreground, though behind I imagined a town, which I discovered while out buying soap, and pretty it was too. Like so many of these old places it was baroque, with Lutheran, Catholic and Evangelical churches. The main town buildings had been spared by the communists although prettier buildings on the edge of town were levelled, leaving only one or two.

The head of the local riding club Stefan Pavel Maksi was my guide – after I'd scrubbed up.

'Total liquidation!' he said. He spoke French. 'The communists were anti-culture and they destroyed anything of beauty which represented another age. Things like the Bolshoi Ballet are just masks over a stupid face; one which wished to ruin anything it could lay its hands on.' There were Russian soldiers hanging round the streets, in their jack-boots and big forage hats.

'No one here will really believe in democracy until they have gone,' he said. 'They're due to go in 1991. The Russians ruined the face of our country and expect to walk away free leaving us to pick up the pieces, and then, and *then* expect us to clothe them and feed them because they can't do it themselves.'

I found I liked Czechoslovakia and the people were very jolly, even Stefan, in spite of his cutting views about Russians. The town was clean, the hotel was clean, clean and efficiently run, more so than Bulgarian places I'd stayed in, and indeed the Czechs regarded the Bulgarians as cultureless. There were plenty of gypsies too, though they were regarded as a menace and once again, I heard of policies for sterilisation; gypsy women were offered 2,000 krona for the treatment.

Stefan waffled on about problems in Czechoslovakia since Havel had taken power. Labour problems, jobs had gone, a lot of the old bureaucratic numbers had been wiped out: money that had been available for social welfare was no longer available, young girls were turning to prostitution, bread that had been two krona a kilo before the revolution was now six krona, and wages had not gone up.

We were sitting with another fellow as Stefan talked: he spoke French and chipped in:

'Lenin was a moron, you know,' he said suddenly.

'I thought he was supposed to be some sort of intellectual,' I answered.

'Nah, course not, anyone who's stupid enough to think a whole society will put the interests of the state before its own has got to be a moron. And the utopia he dreamed of? There never was one except for the Red Bourgeoisie: the rest of us got landed on our arses and not only that but what we had left – old buildings, culture – the commies pulled down as well; look around you. I don't believe there were ever any men who had a vision of a bright new future, I just don't believe it. I don't believe that anyone dreamed of dismantling the old to replace it with a shining new world of order and equality: no, they were just a bunch of bitter old peasants out to ruin anything they could lay their hands on, and that included almost everything. Just think of it, if they'd been honest, why did they need to imprison us behind an Iron Curtain? Which honest society ever needed to contain its people? The only reason, and we all knew it, was because we were having to pay for them to wreak the chaos they did while the rest of the world was forging ahead without us.'

I told him about the old villages in Romania where the people seemed to be living the good life, no stress, no bank managers, no mortgages.

'It stinks', he said. 'And it stinks because it's stagnant, and stagnancy is the hallmark of communism, that and filth. There was no way forward for anybody because the state was run by fools who wanted their cake and to eat it and so they did: big cakes and this is all it's amounted to. Gorbachev isn't the architect of change: he's the instrument of chaos: communism finished because it couldn't go on, not because Gorbachev came along to change it. No, I don't believe Gorbachev, no one does: we're not fooled. And now? Czechoslovakia is communist in all but name: we've still got the same bunch of crooks skulking around at the top. Yes, okay, Havel isn't, but the system these devils left behind is cast iron. Our biggest problem is to break the grip they had on our thinking and if we want to join the West we'll have to think differently. You know, we can't do business yet with the West not only because we haven't got any money, but because we've no idea how to run a business, and guess why?'

His eyes flashed. This was one angry bloke.

'All the produce of Eastern Europe, and what pitiful scratching Russia could churn out, went to pay for guns, bombs, May Day parades, as we starved. And there were English intellectuals who believed in that? You should have shot them.' He had a swig of his drink. There was no stopping this guy.

'Communism,' he said finally. 'Communism was the biggest fraud that has ever swept the face of the earth. And you know what I think? I think they'll still manage to pull something nasty on us: like a ferret, like the last fart of a ferret.'

'The last fart of a ferret?'

'You know, when a ferret's cornered it lets out a filthy stink. The commies are the same.'

Up Between the Toes

We left Rimavska Sabota at eight o'clock on a compass bearing of 270 degrees north which took us across a newly harvested field. It's good going after harvest: you can go on the old straight track for miles and miles. It was a good run from there to Poltar, though we got snarled up in woodland and then got caught out in the collective because they'd got bovine TB, and understandably, didn't want us to stay. However, the agricultural engineer Paul something or other – never got his surname – and a mate with a black eye took me by car to an old friend's place to get us fixed up. The old fellow lived right out in the countryside, and he was just wearing a pair of grubby underpants.

He was bleary-eyed and this was six in the evening. He poured vodka all over the table. '*Nasdravye!*' he grunted, swallowed half a glass then poured again, this time managing to get the glasses. I went back with Paul for the horses, rode back and then we all went out for a night on the town. Happily the old man found something to cover his underpants with, but he was a terrible old soak. His wife had left him and he was going downhill fast. He didn't care about democracy or communism, or Englishmen or horses or anything: he just wanted to be in oblivion, and that's where we left him when we got back to his place at elevenish. Paul and I laid him out in his pit like a corpse, while the horses grazed his lawn or whatever it was outside. He was hitting rock bottom that old boy, needed a bit of AA.

We cleared off early next morning and wandered through low hills, winding up in Ruzina, a big touristy lake with speed boats, wind surfers, paddle boats and water deep enough to swim the horses. That evening we were in Podkrivan having been led there by a little girl who pitched up out of the bushes and simply got on Karo as I was leading him. She left us in Bukovinket where we were guests of a family who left me completely alone, just bringing something to eat into my room and the horses were left outside to graze.

They offered me a bath and I jumped at it: I needed one.

I was given soap, and a towel, led down into a dark place, and told to stand still. I heard this bloke fumbling around, then a light went on and I found myself looking at six cows. In front of them was a tub, with taps, and amazingly, hot water. My host washed the tub out roughly, shrugged his shoulders and left me to it.

It was pretty basic in there and I wondered where to undress, where to hang my clothes. On the cows? I turned on the hot tap and water poured steamy and yellow into the tub. I undressed, hanging my clothes up on a cobwebbed nail beside these cows and wondered whether I should have just flung them over them after all, like clothes horses, clothes cows. And I might tell you it makes you feel pretty silly undressing in front of cows, eyeing you up with their big liquid eyes, sort of half-embarrassed and puzzled, as though you shouldn't be there. You're left wondering what's going through their minds. Anyway, I got into the tub and gazed up as they gazed down. My audience shuffled from foot to foot. There were long eyelashes, tongues up noses, tongues trying to reach you, swishing tails, torrents of dung.

I think, though I'm not certain, but I think the bath doubled as a hayrack which made me wonder how the cows felt about people suddenly throwing all the hay out, filling the thing up with hot water, tearing all their outer layers off and jumping in. Whatever they might have felt, they appeared resigned to it. In fact they seemed to like it; in fact they reminded me of a line of female vocalists on 'Top of the Pops' all standing in a row and swaying, about to burst into song – a sort of bovine bath-time lullaby. It was very cosy. I liked it. Just, it was a touch steamy, that's all. But I could see the sense of it, particularly in winter.

The snag was getting out because I'd gone and left my towel out of reach so had to pad across the floor, which was, well, as floors are where cows are – up between the toes stuff – cold.

As I dried I wondered what things those cows might have witnessed in there because they didn't take their eyes off me from the minute I went in to the minute I left.

Nevertheless it was good to be clean despite smelling more than I did when I went in, but everyone stank so no one gave a hoot.

I wandered around.

The house itself was fairly typical of many farmsteads I'd seen in Czechoslovakia: substantial.

The buildings were wattle and daub for the greater part, with attractive rooflines, with small round-edged tiling, very soft earthenware colours, yellows and fawns.

The houses were more sophisticated than many I'd stayed in, although the cow-bathroom was unusual, and I hadn't come across one like it either before or since. And generally speaking the villages were more up-together, even than many in Hungary. And in Divin, near the lake at Ruzina, I saw a bottle bank, which amazed me. I even bought a pair of shorts in one village, Cinobana, a smallish place – you could never have got shorts in a village in Bulgaria.

And as to the language, it's sort of Slav, but the word 'yes' is 'ah-no', frequently abbreviated to 'no' and is devilish confusing. So you ask about a kon-dom and the man says 'no' so you push off, leaving him with raised eyebrows and half a mile later realise he said yes.

The ride away towards Zilina was classic, through high country with streams and little wells. We went across a saddle of land with a view either side and that was Eden and fogged in the distance, blue as the bloom on a damson, were the Tatra Mountains.

We didn't see a soul on that ride. At once it reminded me of Umbria, the Apennines and Turkey, Turkey because of the old crumbling castle on the lake at Ruzina and what looked like a garrison chateau, a romantic building with towers on each corner, but the Babel of language condemned me to ignorance of what I gazed upon, so I walked past the bolted door, looked up at the castle and thought of Turkey.

It was beautiful country, the people helpful and kind, and it seemed to me that having managed so well under the thumb of communism boded a future pregnant with potential. I was told the Minister of Finance wanted to change things swiftly, to break up the collectives, hand back land to former owners, sell it off. But as the fellow with Stefan pointed out, all that is only possible if you are a people who fundamentally understand the principles of self-determination.

It was a long walk that day: we did well.

PUŞA: Puff, puff, what a slog. Boiling hot. Look at old Fishface sweating out in front. What's he sweating for?
KARO: He's pulling me.
PUŞA: Pulling you?
KARO: Yes! It's easy. When he's walking, drag your feet a bit and he'll pull you.
PUŞA: Like this! Yes, I see! What a good idea ... By the way, I've been thinking. You know what it is about Fishface, don't you?
KARO: No?
PUŞA: He hasn't got a home. I mean, if he had, we'd have got there by now, *surely*! What rotten luck it was to get mixed up with him.
KARO: He's better than the gypsies.
PUŞA: He is a gypsy
KARO: Nhnn...nhnn...nhnn...nhnn...nhnn...

1 September 1990
Down through a woodland, we passed a small stream rippling with weed, cool in the sun. The great growing days are over, fruit drops from trees, apple-bouncing to the earth in front of us and always spotted by the goblins. Not one bouncing apple has been left uneaten on our path. And the plums I pick from the trees as we go beneath, I share with them, and quince, furry in branches.
Look at the rowan, red on the mountain! Autumn moves about the trees turning the emerald of the leaves to topaz, amber and the changing colours of quartz. The fields are bare. Or ploughed.

PUŞA: See this tree coming up? We passed this two hours ago.
KARO: So we did.
PUŞA: Wherever we're going no doubt we'll get there in thousands and thousands of small circles.
KARO: If we ever get there at all.

PUŞA: Be a help if you knew *two* songs.
KARO: Nhnn...nhnn...nhnn...nhnn...nhnn...

Gavin

I telephoned England while in Rimavska Sabota. It cost more to ring England from Czechoslovakia than it had from Bulgaria, which is odd, since Czechoslovakia is closer. Still, it was cheaper to telephone my mother from Bulgaria than it was for me to telephone her from where I live, seventy miles away, so in a way, I wasn't surprised. It had been expensive to ring from Hungary; and from Romania it was impossible – unless you felt like spending all month hanging round a telephone in one of the rare post offices. Trying to get through to Bucharest was bad enough. I tried once and didn't bother again.

Anyway, I got through to Chumpie and asked where and when I was supposed to meet Gavin. She said two things. Gavin asked her:

Could he bring his pyjamas?
Would there be whisky and water at night?

Gavin's a very sensible fellow.

I imagined his luggage already: huge leather trunks all tied up in ropes with this and that like some sea captain's chest, and canvas, shepherd's crook, huge boots, woolly socks, huge hat. I wondered if he'd bring a sheepdog, sheep even.

When I reached Zvolenska Zlatina he was already en route for Zvolen station. He would be coming via Prague, Zlatina, Banska Bystritsa and ultimately Zvolen. It was going to be a bit of a hit and miss affair. Difficult for him since he would be crossing Europe carrying a saddle, saddlebags and all his clobber, and it's one hell of a long way from west to east Czechoslovakia alone.

Still, the idea of meeting him with horses from a train appealed to me, despite my misgivings about train travel.

I pitched up at Club Ierde in Zvolenska Zlatina where there were thirty-odd horses eating their bedding. The club was better heeled than

168

the last place but the horses were standing about in those stables bored out of their minds.

My two friends grazed about outside for a few hours before being put into the barn for the day's wait until Gavin arrived. I went to stay in the Motel Lubica, affiliated to the riding stables, and run by an Italian-speaking entrepreneur called Marian Varga. He was trying to make a go of this out-of-the-way place, and had satellite television which played pop music all day and all night. And if anything sets a couple of cultures apart it's those who want to listen to that rubbish all day and night and those who don't.

Marian was also setting up riding holidays, since, with fifteen horses and all that unfenced countryside, the lake with water-skiing only thirty kilometres away, he was sitting pretty. It's only four days by train from London and actually you can book right through to Zvolenska Zlatina station, but I don't know how easy or difficult it is. Marian planned to charge ten quid a day, bed, breakfast and riding – which seemed pretty reasonable. No doubt that'll change.

Marian had about him exactly the same air as money-minded business types back home. Doubtless he'll make himself a packet, but he's a new breed in Eastern Europe.

I telephoned Chumpie again from Zvolen and she said Gavin would probably be in Zvolen later on, so Marian and I went to meet the Bratislava connection and when we arrived I looked up the platform and there was this gaunt figure with bags over his shoulders, chatting up a few students. I hollered and went over. He greeted me as if I was some wayward dog who's managed to get himself tangled up in barbed wire, then dumped the saddle on me and we drove back to Marian's place chatting about trains, how efficient German ones were, how impressive the Germans were generally, how chaotic the Czech trains, how stupendous Prague was but what a dead atmosphere it had, like a town in curfew.

Gavin I have known for quite a few years and I know that he likes spartan things. Or at least so I thought. I was fairly sure he'd dislike Marian's hotel, but there wasn't another and we didn't have to stay there forever. Besides, as Eastern European hotels go, it was pretty good, it just wasn't attractive or appealing. The village of Zvolenska Zlatina itself isn't unattractive, having low decorative buildings, similar to those in Transylvania. But there was this big ugly restaurant in the middle and a modern sculpture unsympathetic to the tone of the place. And coming to it from Zvolen you pass a huge Walt Disneyed castle which must owe a lot to a civic body whose ideas of restoration were pretty bizarre, to say the least. Motel Lubica is a disappointment because it's just dull, although it sits in a pretty valley. Inside you walk straight in to half a dozen gaming machines all making stupid noises, operated by individuals also making stupid noises. In other words, it combined the worst of any selection of half-beat English pubs but without the rapport.

I explained to Gavin it was a bolthole and, as bolt holes go in Eastern Europe, wasn't bad. You say things like that when you come across hotels or camping sites because it's a relief to be able to stay in them and have a bit of privacy and not have to explain yourself all the time. So we stayed. Gavin sorted out his enormous pile of luggage and I clutched the money Pelham had agreed to fork out, which saved my bacon, temporarily.

Gavin was anxious to see the horses, and said, kindly, he thought they were in good order only I fussed over them too much. But, he conceded, he understood because all he worried about was Mrs Pig at home, whom he also confessed to loving with all his heart and had stayed her execution many a time.

'I just can't bring myself to kill her! I love her! I understand her, she's so *nice!*'

He was desperately concerned that in his absence his wife would have her butchered, and this worried him greatly.

'I'd go mad!'

He also had 'little 'uns' though didn't say it like that – and his wife – and thought about them a lot too. I thought I'd better say that.

Anyway, we stayed in the hotel, clearing off as soon as we could, a day or so later.

Knight

3 September 1990
I forgot to record a couple of mornings ago I performed a duty long overdue. On behalf of and in the absence of Her Majesty The Queen and Ministers of The Crown, on behalf of and in the absence of Court Officials and Officers of Her Majesty's Government I took it upon myself to acknowledge and reward services rendered by one of Her Majesty's loyal subjects (albeit of foreign descent) for his singular deeds and accomplishments. Accordingly, in full cognisance of the gravity of the moment, with proper ceremony such as circumstances might allow, I awarded Karo the K.C.M.G. I awarded him this High Honour for patience, for gentlemanly conduct and gallantry in moments of peril, for distance covered and for hardships borne, for forbearance exhibited in the face of constant batterings from Puşa for the past one and a half thousand kilometres.

I dubbed him with a shovel, both shoulders.

Knight of The Gutter, (First Class).

SIR KARO: Kindly call me God.
PUŞA: (Sigh)

Sir Karo's first duty was to accommodate Gavin and his huge pile of clobber on his portly back and carry him through Zvolenska Zlatina towards Banska Bystritsa. This he did, with complaint. Gavin had too much baggage. The bedroll stood nine inches above the saddle, consisting largely of a wafer of plasticised foam, designed to even out a night's uncomfortable bedding. I knew it wouldn't work on sight. What, however, was more amazing was Gavin did too, but insisted on carrying the wretched thing much to Sir Karo's annoyance.

We left our lodgings, Marian's hotel and The Club Ierde late – at about ten or so, watched pitifully by a group of onlookers who advised us to go left of Banska Bystritsa on account of the high mountains.

The high mountains on the right, we were told, were impassable.

They ought to try the ones on the left some time.

Nevertheless we made good going out of the village, Gavin being happy to be away from the hotel and its satellite television which played pop music non-stop from dawn to dusk back to the next dawn and where groups of carousers shrieked and cackled all night, affording those of us who tried to doss in the place no sleep. By now I was accustomed to this and knew full well that in any Eastern European hotel of any kind of standard, if everything else is apparently okay, you will be denied any kind of kip, somehow or other. The distractions vary from yapping dogs, cock-a-doodle-doing cockerels, cats, and nuns with bells, monks with bells, drunks, partygoers and givers and now, satellite televisions.

Gavin rubbed his eyes and told me he'd shouted at some of the three-o'clock-in-the-morning yellers who responded by muting their mirth for only half an hour.

'I thought it was you!' he accused. 'I was sure I heard your voice.'

'No: I was listening to you shouting at them.'

'Kerr's Pink!' Gavin exclaimed, changing the subject.

'Kerr's Pink?'

'Potatoes! Look at them! I go miles for those potatoes at home, miles! Why haven't we been given any potatoes?'

We had, the day before.

'We have, yesterday.'

'Those weren't potatoes!'

End of conversation. Clearly my knowledge of potatoes is limited. I could have sworn they were potatoes. They were called potatoes, were addressed as '*kartoffi normaal*' by the waiter and I thought, tasted of potatoes. I kept quiet. When in the presence of experts, it's wise to do so.

'Ohhh, *kartoffi normaal*!' Gavin sang at the top of his voice, 'Give me a plateful of *kartoffi normaal!*'

I've never been in the company of anyone who was obsessed with potatoes before.

'That was a rotten breakfast,' he went on. 'Why can't they make a decent breakfast?'

Obsessed with food. I made a mental note to keep an eye open for The Ritz.

The way along was pretty and in the river fat trout glided about through weed. It was a warm day and the mountains in the distance looked friendly, though our first night turned into a trial. As the day ended we were looking for somewhere to stay when we saw three mounted horsemen in the distance. We rode over to them, which involved crossing a heavily-polluted river, then an aerodrome where helicopter trials were in progress, then a railway line, main trunk road and a village.

'I tell you, man, this is no riding country. Look at this lot!' Gavin snorted.

The horses behaved badly too and when we met the three riders they were about as enthusiastic to meet us as one is to discover a wart on one's person. Reluctantly they led us off to a place where a friend kept a few horses and calves. We hung around there until it was obviously hopeless, saved by the local vet who found us a stable, put us up for the night and got my papers stamped – which I was told to do at the border as well as get them stamped by police, but that was far too much of an effort, so made do with the horse papers and left it at that.

In the morning it rained and later that day we were stuck in the middle of nowhere in drizzle, having a thoroughly rotten time and what with Gavin agonising about not having any potatoes, asking why I hadn't fixed accommodation up beforehand, Karo sulking because of the baggage, I wondered how much fun this had suddenly become.

And the mountains for me became another trial. Maybe because I'd been through so many like them, but colour disappeared from my vision and we seemed destined for a deadly world of deadly grey.

'Trees! Can't see! Weather's filthy, what's the point? Ooohh, and imagine, eggs, charred on the outside! And porridge! Why can't we have any porridge?'

SIR KARO: This bloke sings and whistles exactly the same songs as Fishface.

PUŞA: Must be their National Anthem.

SIR KARO: And he's got too much clobber, and he doesn't walk enough, and he's too heavy.

PUŞA: You leave it to me, I'll think of something.

'Haven't seen a man in a decent pair of workboots yet,' Gavin said out of the blue, before he left. 'Look at them all!'

There they were struggling to keep their feet dry. The labourers all work cheap town shoes. You can't get decent boots in those countries. I know: I'd tried. My boots were frayed at the edges from constant wear and were beginning to let in water.

'And look at all this waste! Look at all this concrete! Never seen such a throw-away society!' We passed the usual concrete electric poles on a roadside, and a few steel girders dropped off.

Gavin blew a whistle.

'Change ends!' he bawled out.

'There's no women: you don't see attractive women. There's pretty little girls, then fat women.'

He had a point there. 'Ahh,' he went on, 'when an Italian girl says "*ciao*", I love to hear it, the intonation they get into it, it means "see you tomorrow, same time."'

We stopped for the evening at a small hut conveniently placed by the track, with a stable for three horses, a quantity of hay, and place for us. We'd been thumping around in woodland all afternoon, soaking wet, cold and miserable and at times like that you remember the famous Ronald Reagan quote of 'see one tree and you've seen 'em all', and you begin to believe him.

We lit a campfire, using my flat kettle for hot water, which I hadn't used since I'd been with Chumpie back in the rain in Bulgaria. It was full of soap. Gavin was appalled.

'How can you put soap in a kettle?'

I explained I never used the thing

'But how? Why not?' I told him I rarely lit fires. I don't need endless cups of tea: besides, I never had any.

'But you're so badly organised. Why don't you carry food, water?'

Again I explained. I did carry food, but only a tiny amount: enough for a snack for me. Water I never carry because it's heavy stuff to cart around and besides I would never take a drink without the horses being able to have one first. The chances are if you carry water, you drink and forget about the horses. I won't do that.

Gavin found a small spring, and with the last tiny dribble of whisky he'd been carrying, poured it into a mug. He nodded and grinned. 'The water's champagne. I tell you, the quality of the whisky depends on the water. Try.' He was right. The snag is half a swig of whisky isn't enough for me and I immediately crave more. We didn't have any; happily.

So we wound on next day and the day after, Gavin addressing the passers-by in Swahili: *'Jambo! Habari? Ah! Asanté sana! Mzuri-tu!'*

It's something I understand – both the language, that is, at least in snatches, and the urge to speak it to foreigners. We were stuck for language in Czechoslovakia since we didn't have a dictionary. I'd tried to get one and failed, as had Gavin. And although the language was Slavic, my memory of Bulgarian was washed away by Romanian and Magyar. The only thing I could remember with certainty was kon-dom, and got hold of 'no' meaning yes.

So we were constantly baffled by what anyone said and Gavin's Swahili did little to ease our confusion. But I'm sure it gave him the satisfaction of saying something which sounded foreign at least, even if I was the only one who got his drift.

The horses behaved differently. Puşa, full of everything, endocrine system running to gloss her as fine as a racehorse, whipped along, snorting, prancing, rattling forward. Sir Karo slapped along complaining about Gavin, Gavin's baggage, the distance, the road, the mud, the fog, the rain, country, climate, company – and he sulked. And I was feeling down. We'd hit a northern atmosphere and it was difficult.

We spent a night in a mountain hay barn. It was cold. Gavin lit a fire again, the horses grazed, then walked into this improbable building and started on the hay, of which there was a mountain. Gavin and I planned to sleep in the loft, and failed. A chilly morning light got us out of our fleabags, wearily.

'I would never have believed it,' Gavin gasped. 'That horse has eaten non-stop all night.'

I'd told him Sir Karo had a formidable appetite. He kept him awake because of the snorts, bumping, grunting, piddling and groaning.

For me, it's the chewing.

'That's the last time I sleep with you, *bwana*,' Gavin said to Sir Karo as we rode away down the rest of the mountain to Zilina, where Gavin was to leave and go back to England. It had been a short visit: we travel in different ways, seek different things, have different demands. Maybe it was because I'd been alone so long with the horses I'd become possessive of them, anxious about them. Maybe it was because Gavin demanded to know more of the route so we'd got maps, and usually, I'd hardly bother with maps – you can't tell anything from a map. And when we'd got them and tried to follow them, we'd wound up going round and round trying to find forestry tracks and little signs and gone here, there and everywhere, except forward.

8 September 1990, Zilina.

I am out of clothing. My jersey's in Bulgaria, chaps in Romania, socks in Hungary, my trousers are crutchless, it's Saturday and everything's shut.

My poncho I wear as protection against the wind is a poor substitute for wool. I think of my cupboard at home and the jerseys lying idle there: an old favourite, a pink cashmere full of patches: my gypsy waistcoat, all buttons. For the want of those simple things I'm cold. From late May to a few days ago the temperature rarely left the 90s. Now it's 40 and I'm caught out and haven't got the money.

And going north things are different. Somehow the people have become more cool. It's getting trickier; we the homeless horsemen less palatable, our saddlebags and horse hair not interesting. We're hitting the twentieth century and the new world: we've left the old behind and for us, it's harder, we're no longer drawn in. Is it worth it?

PUŞA: I've got it!
SIR KARO: Got what?
PUŞA: Revenge.
SIR KARO: Revenge?
PUŞA: Roll! With all the luggage on! Wait until he gets off then roll! They'll blame themselves if you roll with all the luggage on! You can really cause some damage *and* get away with it!

This morning, Sir Karo rolled all over Gavin's baggage. Gavin turned his back for a few minutes, disappeared, swallowed a lightning coffee with some roadside friends and returned to find Sir Karo standing with the saddle and bags dangling beneath his belly like trailing intestines. Food squashed, plastic things broken, bottles burst.

SIR KARO: Touche!
PUŞA: Ha!

We arrived in Zilina in late afternoon in pouring rain and within two days had split up. I left Gavin eating breakfast in the hotel dining room. I went up to the horses who were on a collective three kilometres outside town.

I'd thought of taking a truck. The weather was conspiring against me, I'd lost a lot of heart, lost enthusiasm to go on and even though Gavin had kindly brought out more money for me I didn't have the heart to go on. I'd had it with Czechoslovakia, with the rain, the cold indifference of the people, the hardness of their hearts. Both Gavin and I had been appalled to see one old woman stripping nettles by hand to make soup, because the state bread truck had failed to arrive again. It was another example of Czechoslovakia being communist still in all but name: that the desire to change from communism to democracy was lost in the psyche of the people whose thinking was communist and impossible to break.

I got to the collective, looked at the grey wind-swirling mountains, and wondered if I should have gone home with Gavin.

It's difficult going on sometimes.

A Promise

Gavin was with me for a week or so in Czechoslovakia, in time to celebrate his birthday, which is on 7 September but which, by dint of not knowing what the date was, we celebrated a day late, on the 8th, with pork fat.

'What's this?'

'Pork fat.'

'I asked for bacon.'

'That's it.'

'This isn't bacon!'

'No: it's fat.'

'What do they do with the pig? Throw it away? Poor Mrs Pig!' He looked heart-broken, staring with pain at the greasy offering on his plate, torn between not eating it but dying for something, and riddled with misgivings about Mrs Pig at home and what fate might have befallen her.

'Poor Mrs Pig!' he said again shoving the fat to one side.

'Why can't they make porridge?' He looked around to see what anyone else might be eating.

'They're all at it!' And with a huge sigh, dropped his fork and resigned himself to a basket of stale bread.

An hour later we were on the horses in the steamy morning and he was singing.

'Oooh, *kartoffi normaal*! Oohh, why can't they make porridge!'

Although for the greater part of the time Gavin was with me we seemed to be riding in rain or thick woodland, we rode through spectacular country. I remember the sun on the plain between the ring of mountains, the Fatra and Tatra, and that morning's ride up the valley between the two where mist and cloud rolled in dark dimples in these great mountain ranges, like huge curtains drawn across the edges of some vast and strangely-lit stage. The villages we passed were silent and orderly, with yellow churches and shut *bufets*. Old men hoed weeds, women turned up potatoes.

'Potatoes!'

When we were in Zilina I was interested in Gavin's reaction to the town. We went to find a restaurant: it was Saturday night, 8.30.

'Everything's shut! Is there a curfew? There's not a soul about, no taxis, no streetlights, no police: nothing! It's dead. Where's the centre to this place?'

It was like a ghost town. We found a restaurant, which was like a ghost restaurant, and the food lousy. Then on another occasion, when taking a bus to the stables outside Martin, Gavin pointed out a deal going on between the bus driver and a passenger. A Big-Cheese backhander went into the glove box. Gavin winked. 'I wonder how much of that goes on?'

In a way it was good to see with another pair of eyes and though I was sorry to see him go, I was also glad to be alone again, alone with the horses, though I was far from happy about carrying on. My money was low, it was a long way to England and I'd been in the saddle for longer than I had originally anticipated. The journey seemed to have gone flat and I wondered about chucking it in.

PUŞA: Do you hear that? Fishface is talking about going home.
SIR KARO: What about us? What will happen to us?
PUŞA: Where will we live?
SIR KARO: Who will feed us?
PUŞA: Who will look after us?
SIR KARO: What will happen?
PUŞA: He's going to sell us!
SIR KARO
He can't! He can't! He promised!
PUŞA: He promised!

179

As I was debating what to do, I had the horses shod again, using the same shoes that were put on way back in Hungary. The blacksmith had a dry line in observations. There was a girl in the stable when the shoes were going on and she translated. I asked what the blacksmith thought of democracy. He straightened his back and waving a horseshoe at me answered, 'Tell me what democracy is and I'll tell you what I think of it.'

I asked what would happen to the collectives now Czechoslovakia was supposed to be democratic.

'Ninch!' He said. Nothing.

'Of Havel? What do you think of Havel?'

'He's a writer.'

'And?'

'He's a writer.'

I looked out of the cobwebbed window at the rain. I didn't feel like tackling those mountains at all, the very thought of going on was a nightmare: I was fed up with mountains. On the map they looked huge, strung along with a valley full of cranes and lorries. I looked back at the horses. How could I leave them? But how could I take them? I had 650 dollars and reckoned England two to three months' ride at least. At its most generous that was about ten dollars a day and didn't include incidentals like shoeing, fixing visas, the possibility of quarantine or transport across the Channel, which I knew would be at least 200 pounds, nearly half my money. One way or another, it didn't look as if I was going to make it. Pelham had already given me more than they agreed to and things looked bleak. Somewhere along the line I was going to have to sell the horses.

But I don't like selling horses. And, besides, there was something else.

You might remember the mountains in Romania, about a night when we were caught out? I said something happened in those mountains and that I'd tell you about it later? Well this is it.

Shortly after André left I was up in the mountains with Karo and Puşa and we were caught in rain. We were in thick woodland and night was falling. Under the trees it was wet and the tiny path we'd followed so faithfully had dwindled to nothing beneath our feet; we were confounded, homeless, hungry and soaked. We'd gone too far to turn back and I didn't know how much further that forest went on. I felt pretty scared. You know, those forests in Transylvania are huge and very lonely places.

Night closed around us in a web and darkness sneaked about cold and mean. We were frightened, the three of us. It was a very eerie place and bushes seemed to move the way they do at nightfall, when you're alone. All was silent but for the rain and the wind and murmur of the trees.

And there, in that darkness I held Karo's and Puşa's heads close to mine. I could see their eyes straining, the white at the edges, and steam rising off their flanks even as the darkness deepened and rain hissed in the trees. And as I held their heads close to mine, I felt their breath in my face and felt their fear and uncertainty, and I wanted to end their fear and uncertainty, and made them a promise, and the promise I made them was this. I promised them that I would take them to my home. I promised them they wouldn't have to walk any more, that I would take their shoes off and they could play and graze in the green fields that look over the changing colours of the Beacon, where the streams lie, south-facing, in the eye of the sun.

In winter I would cook them hot barley and put jackets on them at night when it was cold. I promised them they would live in the old stone barn with Gonzo, my Criollo gelding, and Dolly, a dapple-grey Welsh who belongs to my friend and neighbour Alan Watkins. I promised Puşa that when her time came, she could have her foal in the old barn and I would find a name that would be a reflection of her, the journey she made and the land she came from, and I promised Karo that he would never be afraid again. This was the promise I made to my horses that night in Transylvania.

For the rest of that night we stood together in the darkness in silence as the trees tossed their heads and the storm raged about us. Then, as the first hint of dawn struck the night sky as dim as the coat of an iron-grey, I took a reading on my compass from its tiny tritium light and we went down through the trees into a deepening chasm and stones rolled away wet beneath us. We followed that tiny light all the way, weaving through the forest until the sky and trees filled with day and at noon we burst into a green and shining world with flying fields and distant blue hills.

There we stopped. Karo and Puşa grazed for two, three hours and I hung clothes and saddlecloths out to dry, then in the afternoon, we went on.

But the promise was made, and whatever the odds set against us, I steeled myself to honour it.

When the horses were shod in that barn in Czechoslovakia, I saddled them, put the pack on Puşa, left the maps on a wall and we went out into the rain, to Poland.

Rafał

The last couple of days in Czechoslovakia were marked by heavy rain. The border was about seventy kilometres from Zilina and the hills that looked so grim from the map were lovely and gentle and forested. I passed the night with a gypsy family, the last gypsies I stayed with, and they were wretched in every respect. Their home was as miserable as a cave, and yet they, who must have been the poorest people in the village were the ones who gave me and my ponies shelter. And they exemplified something I have found from my journeys with horses that the poorer the people, the more likely they are to help and the poorer the country the kinder the people. Why is this?

I approached Český Těšin, my exit point according to my visa, on the main road, a swirling lorry-bedevilled, juggernauted nightmare, and that road, like the road I remember over the Alps, was trafficked by vast lorries with cargoes of horses destined to become salami, and that's a wicked trade, racked with cruelty.

I tried for a night's lodging in the agricultural college in Český Těšin but had no luck. It was 5.30 in the evening, we were all hungry, all wet and once again, I had no visa, no vet papers, no transit visa, no international transport document, nothing.

I went to the border and crossed the little bridge, queue-jumped all the traffic, tethered the horses to some steel rails, and went into the customs office. They took my passport and vet papers. I was given a cold look. They shook their heads.

'You have no visa.'

'I know. I wondered if you could sell me one.'

'No, we can't. You must go to Ostrava.'

It must have been the bleakness of my expression, but I saw a look of pity in the man's eye as he handed my passport back. Ostrava was thirty kilometres away, not far by car, but this was dusk, night was falling, it was raining again and I was on foot.

Feeling absolutely crushed I returned to the horses and told them

183

we were out of luck, that we'd have to wait, get a bed somewhere in the town, which I'd already tried and failed to find. Nothing can lift you from the disappointment of moments like that except that which has cast you down.

The guards were all watching me, and people in cars, and someone came over to pat the horses, say hello; but I was crushed: I didn't want to go back in to Czechoslovakia: I hate going back. Moments passed and the full weight of disappointment grew on me. I saw only darkness, only things closing in: the shortage of money, distance to my home, the cold, the bleakness of my position, that we had no roof over our heads, were hungry and footsore.

I felt these eyes watching me as I untied the tether ropes and looked back across the bridge to Český Těšin, that dimly-lit little town where there was no bed for us.

A Polish guard came slowly over. I was sure he was going to tell me to get off the bridge because I was holding up the traffic, or tell me I couldn't come in anyway, whatever I did.

'Give me your passport, go through the barrier and into Poland. I'll get you your vet papers and a ten-day visa. Now move!'

I had those horses untied in a flash and hit the barrier before they had time to pick it up. Everything was suddenly full of light. Within fifteen minutes I was issued with a transit visa, vet papers, duty paid and I was in.

'Go seven kilometres down this road,' the same man said, 'following the river. I will meet you outside a village called Dzięgelow, and you can stay with me; we will find somewhere for your horses, we'll feed you and clean you up, all three of you! Now go!'

He spat all this out in a mixture of German and broken English, and I did exactly what he said. Seven kilometres down the road he was waiting for me. He was called Rafał Dziubek and at eleven that night I was sitting with him and his family after a big meal, after having stabled and fed the horses and his warmth and welcome knocked me out clean and I slept better there than I'd slept for months.

I have always liked the Poles having come into contact with a few in England. I remember fondly a Polish carpenter called Vlada who once did some work for my father. He, like so many Poles, had a wonderful broad face with high cheekbones, dark deep-set eyes. He had lines running down his face, and when he smiled the lines angled and made his smile seem bigger. I remember him because he always smelled of sawdust and because my father said he was a damn good carpenter. At school, my music tutor was Polish as was the art master, who was called Otto, and they were both talented. And a friend of mine knew Szikorski, leader of the Polish Airforce who flew out of Britain in the Second World War.

When I told this to Rafał he was abashed, and smiled awkwardly and reinforced everything I've ever thought about Poles. And if the Turks are hospitable and the Romanians hospitable to a fault, then so are the Poles. They'll let you do nothing, offer you everything, see to your every comfort but are not short of spirit.

'One big actor!' Rafał said suddenly.

'Who?'

'Lech Wałęsa!'

'Really?'

'And the Pope! It's what many Polish people think. You know what they've been discussing in government for the past year? They've been arguing about how big the crown on the eagle's head should be! I ask you! It's all we ever hear! They never talk about anything sensible, anything that matters. I expect we'll have Lech Wałęsa voted in as president, but lots of people don't think he's too bright. He's not very wise, you know, and there's this anti-Semitic thing going on. It's dangerous. And we've got ripping inflation, 700,000 zloty three months ago is now equivalent to 1,600,000. What about that?' Rafał bolted his breakfast, waved a hurried goodbye and got into his car.

I had a look around outside when Rafał went back to work. It was pretty. The houses were nice with good big gardens and it all felt a lot more sophisticated than northern Czechoslovakia. The biggest houses were built by people who'd been working overseas and had brought back hard currency, and the currency that had clout, as in Czechoslovakia, as in all of Eastern Europe, was the Deutschmark.

I met Rafi's neighbours, Anna Heczko and her boyfriend Krzystof Kubeczek, an intelligent young couple, and between the three of them they filled in a background of Poland for me. Maps were dug out, scenes of battles argued over, the whereabouts of Hitler's bunkers, talk of the Second World War and I realised then that it was still pretty fresh in the minds of these people. They were afraid of unification because Poland lies between Germany again growing strong and Russia in tatters, though it was the Russians they particularly disliked.

I was with them when the Two Plus Four Treaty was signed in Moscow by Gorbachev, Kohl, Bush and Thatcher. Unification date was set for 4 October 1990 and drew a few comments.

'There is a man called Herbert Czada and he was born in Skoczow, just north of Ciesyn and graduated there. He's now living in West Germany and fighting for Silesia to be incorporated into Germany. He has an organisation which supports him, some 200,000 people and a minority in Poland. It worries us. We've already had disputes over our western border. We have little reason to trust Germany, and none to trust Russia.'

They talked about the new government, the rising tide of democracy.

'Exactly the same people are trying to be democrats today who were communists yesterday!'

'Shows one thing for sure.'

'What's that?'

'They can't have any principles.' Silence, heads shake. 'And Germany gathering strength on the doorstep, Russia imploding, England with mixed leadership problems and America off in some dope-hazed distance – what does it all remind you of?'

'And Japan expanding – invisibly ...'

'And China, dormant but moody ...'

'Yes, but if the Germans did try anything, they'd be jumped on so quick ...'

'Yes, but by whom?'

'How?'

'And the Czechoslovakians and their Velvet Revolution – you know they could pay off their national debt at a stroke? Look at the mess Russia has left us with, the ecological disaster at Katowice!'

'What about Auschwitz?' I asked.

There was a minute's silence.

'I'll take you,' Rafał answered.

I was surprised by Auschwitz on arrival, surprised by the number of German cars in the car park, surprised that it was such a big place, with these huge dark brick buildings, surprised at my own sense of horror, and surprised that having got there, I didn't want to go in.

But I did, and walked round, first wondering why it had been kept as such a hideous museum. The air itself felt shocked: it had a curious, charged feel, disturbed at some deep, deep level, and bitter: and it's chilling walking beneath the gate that reads *'Albeit Macht Frei'*. Work makes you free. Then into the many brickblock buildings – dormitories – of which many have been kept as they were, with drawings, scratchings on the wall. Dear God, the very place seethed with misery, outrage, horror. I didn't know until then the Nazis scalped their victims and used the hair to make clothing, suits. Tens of tons of hair. I didn't know that. Nor did I know that it had been set up expressly for the extermination of the entire Jewish race. That I hadn't realised either. Nor that 4,000,000 people had died there. There were quite a few people wandering around, two Hassidic Jews, Americans, Germans and four Londoners. I read the comment they wrote in the comments book, it read: 'Very saddened by this Hell called Auschwitz: your turn next you murdering Nazi bastards.'

That's what they wrote.

Auschwitz made them angry.

It made me weep.

I don't know what it was that made me weep, what emotion shook me, but I found myself gazing at a photograph of a pretty young girl, eighteen maybe, how big and beautiful her eyes were, what intelligence shone in her face, the appeal in her eye, the loss for an understanding: even the graininess of the photograph couldn't hide the softness of her skin, the line of her eyebrow. What happened to her? What did they do? What crime had she committed?

She was a gypsy. She remained alive for fourteen days. Is there ever a time to forget this? To forgive?

It was she made me weep. What the emotion was I don't know, I can't pinpoint the feeling, the overwhelming sensation that hit my chest. I have tried since to think what it was, but still I don't know. Certainly it was sadness, but I don't know if it was sadness for the lovely gypsy girl or a sadness that men can do what those men did.

I'm not surprised there are still people who continue to hunt them down.

There was another photograph of a young man, twenty. He was a fine looking fellow and had this no messing look about him. He lasted a week, cause of death: 'natural'.

Auschwitz, Treblinka, Belzec, Chelmno and Sobitor were set up as extermination camps. Even before 1939 the Nazis had rounded up and executed 250,000 anti-fascists, executing 32,000 by axe.

The order to set up Auschwitz came in 1942 with Rudolf Hoss to be camp Kommandant. It was to be the biggest camp devoted to the total annihilation of the Jews. But listen to the mind behind it: in 1937 Hitler told the alumni of the SS political school in Sonthofan that 'the German People has the right to control the whole of Europe and transform it into the Teutonic Reich of the German People.' In *Mein Kampf* he wrote, 'the national socialist movement must remove the existing disproportion between the area of our country and the number of its inhabitants', and this was expanded by Alfred Rosenberg who continued – 'we cannot have any consideration for Poles or Czechs . . . they must be pushed eastwards in order to make their lands available for the ploughs of German peasants.'

Orders were given for the extermination of gypsies and a gypsy camp was set up in Birkenau where whole families, women, children, all were sent and they all died of hunger, illness, cold, exhaustion or were murdered in the gas chambers. And in a particularly chilling comment, Hoss wrote of the gypsies left in Auschwitz in August 1944 that 'these had to go into the gas chambers. Up to the last moments they did not know what was happening to them when they went towards crematorium V.

'It was not easy to drive them into the gas chambers.'

Before his execution after the Nuremberg Trials in 1947 Hoss said that 'in the confines of my cell I have come to the bitter realization what atrocious crimes against mankind I had committed .. . I had carried out part of the horrible plans of genocide conceived by the Third Reich and I pay with my life for this responsibility ... I wish and hope that the fact of having disclosed and proved all these horrible crimes will, for ever after, prevent the arising of even the remotest possibility of such atrocities occurring again.'

Eisenhower said: 'the task of those called upon to ensure peace will be to create conditions which will make it forever impossible for the Nazi monster to raise its head.'

And the little booklet you can get at Auschwitz reads: 'Despite the Potsdam Agreement which provided for the complete demilitarisation of Germany there are a number of underground "soldiers unions" in both east and west Germany who are attempting a revisionist programme and their numbers are growing.'

The unification of Germany has put these groups in touch with one another.

Posse of Angels

14 September 1990
Saturday morning. I stayed with Rafał for three nights which hit a hole in my visa expiry time. No chance of making it by foot to the East German border so will have to find some other way. The intercession of St Christopher would be handy, particularly since I've gone and left my small wallet under a tree in Czechoslovakia: I know exactly where. What an Idiot. Now I'm practically skint.

Rafał's sons were anxious to ride Karo and Puşa, as were two little girls and two bigger ones. Anna and I went for a ride in the woods the day before; Sir Karo behaved as his title befits. However this morning, having been in the same stable for a few days both horses were in effusive mood.
Letting them out of the barn they spent the first fifteen minutes high kicking, bucking and snorting – a wilder pair of broncos you've never seen. Puşa booted and pranced while Sir Karo arched his neck and thundered his feet off until the ground shook, both horses roaring their heads off and thrashing the air with their front feet.
'Aren't they nice!' one of the little girls said.
'Hell's bells,' says I.
The little girls were dying to ride. What can you do? You can't say, look they're unrideable, because I was about to ride them, so I tacked them up, which wasn't easy, Karo being a perfect devil to hold while the children giggled about behind those lethal limbs, and more alarmingly behind Puşa, who is known for her backhanders. The horses were snarling. I put two little girls on.
They walked up the road like a couple of beach ponies.
What is it with horses and children?

190

After the rides I set out for the Stadnina Koni at Ochaby, the equestrian centre which was *en route* and not far. Anna and Krys said they thought I might find a truck going west there since voltage competitions were being held. My funds were now at drama level and any mode, any method of getting home I would consider. Having ridden through rain for very nearly three weeks I had 'flu, and my spirit for going on had actually broken in Czechoslovakia. All I wanted to do was get home with the horses, somehow. I'd changed my money and including what Gavin brought out, after the recent discovery I was down to 560 Deutschmarks and a few zloty. About 290 quid. Distance to England, 3,000 kilometres.

Rafał, his two sons, Krys, Krys's sister – one of the pony riders, Anna, Anna's father, two dogs, a cat, two cyclists and of course Sir Karo, Puşa and I left Dzięgelow at eleven on a bright morning. It was quite an entourage, and saying goodbye is always hard, but saying goodbye to Rafał was very hard. Not only had he got me into the country, but he'd stabled the horses, fed us all, taken me to Auschwitz, given me a roof and breathing space, his wife washed and mended my clothes, Rafał had provided Anna and Krys – translators – he'd plied me with wine and brandy and on top of all this, I found him cleaning my boots. With very little English, but the aid of a dictionary 'word programme' he called it, he stuffed a note into my hand as we parted. It read: *'Dajboze Szczescie.* Rafał.D.' and in English beneath, 'Would to God again anew.'

I got the drift, and hoped so.

Krys showed me a cross-country route after the entourage stayed and waved and then someway along this road Krys left me, and again I was alone. He reminded me of Brains in Thunderbirds: with big glasses, the same quick analytic mind. He was a nice fellow.

The road he put us on was winding and gravelly and snaked through the hips of hills, soft and green with trees and grass, where uncut maize moved in the wind like the sea and brick houses snored down in the valleys dark and pink and sleeping. There was a house, like a Cotswold farmhouse – I saw it, up on a hill, and others, not so pretty. Like hens, old women scratched about in the earth, turning up potatoes, and blue-clothed men tinkered with homemade tractors as children wheeled about on bicycles and the sky raced in clouds, dim and grey, threatening rain.

We crossed the main road to Ogrodzona and I rode the lake-lined lane past Kostkowice and Debowiec where moorhens scattered across the water like buckshot.

We arrived at Ochaby at three to find Krys and Anna there. They'd driven. Not only had they driven to meet me but owing to my foreshortened visa and my shortage of funds, they'd fixed for me to be taken by horsebox to Poznan, right up in central Poland, and they'd fixed it for me to go for nothing

All I can say is that in my experience that was typically Polish.

They didn't stay long in the afternoon, just enough time to ensure everything was properly sorted out, that I had a night's billet and then planked me down to watch a very excellent round of voltage. Then they left. They'll be coming to stay with me sometime.

The Stadnina Koni was an impressive place with fifty or so state-owned horses, big roomy stables, tack, jumps, cross-country courses, racetracks – the lot. I hadn't come across anything like it before, at least not so apparently richly endowed and the hotel I was put in was three or so kilometres away, with stabling for the horses and again set up specifically for visiting riders.

I wasn't charged.

The following day one of the competing teams loaded Karo and Puşa on to a box and drove eight hours to central Poland, to Stadnina Iwno, an equally well set up manège, only specialising in breeding. There were a hundred and fifty brood mares there, groups of stallions, thirty permanent live-in grooms, two permanent blacksmiths and the whole was run by the Helak family, who carry considerable weight throughout the Eastern Bloc and Russia for experience with horses, international events, competitions and judging.

The horses were in superb condition and the whole place on first sight looked like some Texan oil billionaire's dream, with landscaped park, a beautiful lake, willows, big airy white stables, clover-rich meadows, peopled by knee-deep brood mares. There was a racecourse, arena and cross-country course. I saw videos of competitions, and though not competitive minded myself, the standard I noticed was high. They were keen to make contact with English clubs and teams and for my part I agreed to make this known back home.

Danuta Helak, the matriarch of it all was revealing about communism and its demise. 'We don't like the Russians,' she said, 'we have little enough reason: their rotten system has all but ruined us and the sad thing is that we have become indoctrinated with their way of thinking, we have developed a kind of Russian mentality. We are not western you know, because we have come to think like Russians: we don't want to, but we do: forty years leaves its mark. Our real problem is one of mentality – and our agriculture? We are over-producers now: we have too much food and the Russians want it, because they don't have enough. But they can't pay. They haven't any money. And you have enough in the West. What is the answer? And Gorbachev? We don't like him either: no one really does in the Eastern Bloc, because we don't see him as the man of change: communism just fell apart and he came along to try to save face. And Raisa? You know we saw her appear on television covered in sparklers: that didn't go down too well.'

'*W Szczebrzeszynie chrzaszcz brzmi w trzcinie,*' Barbara, her daughter-in-law said over dinner. 'See if you can say it.' I couldn't. My tongue stuck to the roof of my mouth. I even had trouble writing it, let alone saying it. It means 'In Szczebrzeszynie the may-bugs sound in the reeds.' Quite. And a joke: If you had the chance, would you rather go to a Russian or American Hell?

The answer: A Russian one because they would run out of heating oil.

The horses were shod again using the Hungarian shoes with a few blobs of weld fore and aft and a day or so later Puşa, Karo and I set off westward.

We had an outrider, a fellow on a big bay, and he rode nicely through the trees down past the lake where a stream was running. The weather was cool, overcast and rain clouds rolled over in the sky. For the first time I stayed on tarmac, which I would never normally have done, but it was because I was going broke and had to find the quickest route. And though the horses were well rested and well fed, looking glossy and bright eyed, they lacked the spirit they normally threw into their stride, and I knew it was coming from me. My enthusiasm had died. As it rained I knew there, beneath that sullen sky and under the dripping trees that the ride was already finished. It was over. I wanted to go home, and I wanted to go home with the horses. I'd set out to ride for three months, or as long as my money held out, but now I'd ridden for nearly six months and was badly overstretched. My Deutschmarks had dwindled further and despite not being charged for the long drive from southern to central Poland, I still had a long way to go and, realistically, I didn't even have enough money to get home myself, let alone with the horses.

Ten kilometres down that road I arrived soaking in a place called Gospodarstwo Kaczyna, another horse place, pointed out to me by the Helaks and I stayed. There was a little horse trailer there too, which I noticed and wondered whose it was. It seemed to me to be the only way on from there.

In their stable that night I looked at Karo and Puşa and tried to count up how many places they'd stayed in, and couldn't. But I remembered places right up in the mountains in Romania, places out in the *putzsa* in Hungary, and that cold night with Karo in the Balkans: all seemed so long ago, so far away, yet every night, barring one, we'd found ourselves a home, somehow, and every night, barring one, we'd found food and water. And those horses hadn't eaten the same thing for two meals running, and often they'd eaten some pretty ropy stuff: we all had, but they looked wonderful and in their eyes you could see glowing confidence, they were bright and clear and even Puşa's blindness had now more or less gone, though her left eye was still cloudy. But every one of their actions, everything they did seemed to me to show a kind of inner strength. They funked nothing and often I'd called on them to cross pitifully insubstantial bridges, or asked them to swim rivers with no visible or obvious exit on the far side and always they'd done it.

And the day before we galloped full tilt around an arena, Puşa and Karo side by side, footfall for footfall. They jumped as one, went up a bank as one, and down the other side as one, we went down into a ditch as one, over a log, then sprung up the other side as one, footfall for footfall, a cross-country course, side by side, no flinching, no funking, everything taken at hard gallop, ears forward.

I had not trained them to be like this.

We had a little audience and I knew we'd impressed them, I knew it by the way they looked at us and by their silence. The horses had been wonderful in that moment and if the long ride was all for nothing, in that moment that they should have done what they did with such apparent ease, then every second I'd been with them had been worthwhile, just for that moment.

I was so proud of them.

Then I put them out on their long tethers and of course, they didn't tangle, they never tangle and these people came to look at them, and pat them, and say 'they might be small and they might be gypsy horses, and they've got no blood, but there's no denying, they're good, they're very, very good.'

How can you leave animals like this? How many times had I felt the soft breath of these horses across my face at night? How many times had I heard them calling to each other, seen them necking, nuzzling one another, seen them pawing the ground, heard that pattern of footfalls, which if there were twenty horses running together I'd know theirs in amongst them. You get to know your horses well when you live with them night and day. And how many times had I tried to sleep as Karo chewed away in my ear, or heard Puşa lie down beside me, or gone out to see them in some strange stable, or felt fear as they felt it when we were confronted by new obstacles, new problems?

I rode them the following morning waiting for the weather to brighten up. I took them out over a piece of flattish land, recently ploughed. We followed a small track, as ever, and all the way a little family of swallows played around us, like some posse of angels, nearly touching the horses. They were a joy to watch, Karo and Puşa flinching as they came that fraction too close, their dark shapes flickering low across the earth, skimming the autumn grass, they, gathering for their long flight south.

When we got back to Kaczyna, I was told that the boss of the place, Franek, would take us to Eastern Germany.

The Gunnery Range

Poland rolled past with its towns strung along the road like worn-out, besieged citadels, tired and lack-lustre, the last great legacy of communism, the people weary of the grind, uninspired and unchallenged, drunks falling around, no-hopers in a world that was rapidly changing.

Franek talked occasionally, but language divided us, though he knew more English than I Russian or Polish. In a way, I was glad not to have ridden. I'd had enough of that, though I still had more to come.

How he got us through the East German/Polish border I don't know. They didn't even look at my passport and laughed at the horses' papers, but stamped them up anyway, which was useful, because that stamp took me right through Germany since the border dividing east and west had just come down, a month or so before unification. Three miles down the road, Franek dropped us off in Höchenwalde, another riding establishment. The Helaks had arranged for them to take us in: it's incredible the influence that family has in Eastern Europe.

And once again, I was welcomed, given a bed by Olaf Hille, one of the stable managers, and billeted in a groom's quarters above another groom's quarters in a quadrangle where the horses were stabled.

Olaf's flat had a western feel about it: western goods on display, washing powders, shampoos, soaps, exotic food – all arrived since the pulling down of the Berlin Wall. It was 24 September, a week or so to unification.

'Cherman beer is ze best beer in ze Vorld!' Rimo exclaimed pouring out a glass. Rimo, the young boss of the place was looking forward to unification because it meant he'd get to sell more horses. They had a sale coming up.

'Ve sell to the Dutch mostly: vun horse, vun good horse maybe two sousand Deutschmarks!' Seven hundred quid: the horses big, sixteen hand jobs, and fair with it. I thought about my diminishing pile of dough: I could afford a leg, perhaps, or a mane, or tail. I looked up into the sky: rain. Why did it always have to rain? I pulled out the money

196

and counted: 200 Deutschmarks, a bit short of seventy quid. Distance to England: one thousand kilometres.

I kept my hysteria to myself. What I needed was a miracle. A sizeable one.

Going into Puşa's and Karo's stable I thought what a mess Karo's mane had become and tried to do something about it, but it still looked dreadful. Puşa's I rehogged, curving it in an arc, like the horses of Greek myths; it's pretty. Should I hog Karo's, I wondered? What would he look like? Nah, I thought: daren't. An hour later I took hold of a chunk of Karo's mane in one hand and with scissors in the other, cut.

Something terrifying about cutting manes: there's no going back. What was I doing? His mane was a fright, but was this the way to treat it? Snip, snip, snip. Karo chewed on. Was he aware of what I was doing? How would he feel about it?

It looked dreadful. My heart hit my boots. What had I done? I tidied it up, and it looked better, but why did he have to look so bald? And these sales about to start! Why did I have to go and cut his mane off just before the sales? All these people were about to come poking round. Why am I such an idiot?

At eleven the sale began, horses arrived from outlying stables: they lined up *right* beside Karo and Puşa. People milled about.

Then a man appeared and stood gazing at Karo and Puşa. He explained he was the manager of the local Bundesbank. He'd been transferred to Frankfurt Oder to set up business ventures, sort out the money, get the economy working. He'd arrived with a staff of seventy. He was enjoying himself.

And he was interested in horses. He liked driving horses and lit on Karo and Puşa instantly. 'They're evenly matched,' he pointed out. I said I knew. Not bad looking, he said, pretty that mare, isn't she? With that big wide forehead and neat little muzzle, hogged mane, those little short cannons to the front and big long shannons to the rear: she's striking, he said. And what's that brand on the other one, 316? Interesting. Do they know harness, he asked. I told him every gypsy horse knows harness. His eyes widened, then. He drifted off, then came back, and drifted off and came back and did that about twenty times. Other people looked. Lots of people.

'I'm prepared to offer you 3,000 Deutschmarks for each horse,' the man hazarded eventually.

I was taken aback, and for one moment thought it would be so easy to accept, just take the money, get on a plane, and go home. He showed me pictures of his home, his horses, nice stables. I told him what Puşa and Karo had done, and yes, they could drive, told you once already, I said, both of them. He raised his eyebrows. What sort of driving? Carts, I told him, they'd both pulled carts. He became more interested and went into the stable, ran his hands over them.

He increased his offer. Then someone else showed interest. The horses were nice, they said, fit and glossy: good for children. Are they good with children? Of course, I said, and they can swim and undo knots – all sorts of funny things. They're wonderful with children. And the mare? Pregnant? Three horses! How much? they asked.

I told them what the Bundesbank man offered. They nodded. Not bad: maybe they'd offer more. Rimo came over, someone else was interested, would I accept 3,500 Deutschmarks for each horse? 7,000 Deutschmarks: that was about 2,300 quid. I thought about my seventy.

I went into the stable – Puşa and Karo always shared a stable: and they came to me and put their noses in my hand, and I showed off a bit maybe, showed what tricks they knew, what little games we could play together. Everybody liked that. Go on! Show us another trick! How much are they? Go on, give us your price!

And so I patted them and looked into their dark eyes and then back at the people and said:

'They're not for sale.'

The man was annoyed. I'd wasted his time. No, I said, the horses had never been for sale: those are the ones for sale over there. Your assumption, I said. He stalked off in a huff; I didn't like him anyway: I didn't like the way he couldn't look at me in the eye, how he always talked to his hands. He couldn't have had those horses, not for 3,000,000 Deutschmarks. They just weren't for sale.

Talk switched: there was a truck going to Hannover, four hundred kilometres. 1,000 Deutschmarks.

End of conversation.

I thought about the British Army in Berlin, the cavalry there and a couple of days later, set out. On horseback.

And Eastern Germany is exactly like the rest of Eastern Europe: it's all big open fields, with no gates, no fences and you can ride from Höchenwalde to Berlin all the way without touching tarmac. We set out in light drizzle and very short of enthusiasm. We found a track going due west and stuck to it. It was a good direction, wandering through ploughed fields and avenues of acacia, then broke into birch woodland, which was the most picturesque woodland I have ever seen, with a carpet of heather which against the silver paper-bark birch was a heady mix. The woodland cleared and we wound up in an open piece of ground full of craters and holes, which we skirted and weaved through. It was a strange place, with a dead feel, and eerie. At the far end there were these green things lined up in front of some low buildings, too far away to make out distinctly. Nah, I thought, can't be, the Russians have all gone, haven't they? I screwed up my eyes to see what they were.

The horses were jumpy. What was the matter with the horses? Staring down into one of these craters I thought they hadn't been made by machines at all. I looked back at the green things, then gave Karo a pretty big boot because I was beginning to get a nasty feeling about this place, and he didn't need a lot of encouragement. Puşa slapped up behind, then came right up head-to-head with Karo and they started to pull on pretty strong and so there I was trying to calm them down getting more and more edgy about this place when there was an almighty flash from one of these green things, a hell of a wallop and that shell went screeching up over our heads, and we were off!

We went scattering across the rest of that plain with these tanks firing away at the far end and shells exploding about a hundred yards away from us and each time they exploded we felt the shock, the impact in the air and it made those ponies shift.

I was ducking branches, half trying to slow them down, half wanting them to go faster, and I know Karo well enough to know he won't let a snaffle stop him when he's got it in his teeth and those horses fairly knackered me, Karo with his head between his knees going full-bore and me hanging across his back scared to death of being smashed up, and I tell you, if we'd gone that speed all the way we'd have been back in England in time for dinner.

Instead we came screeching up in a big froth at a camp where the Kommandant – I suppose – was screaming his head off about everything being *verboten*, and this and that and something about *minen*, but the horses were far too lathered up to stand still so off we shot again, with shells booming away about a kilometre behind and those two kept up the same speed, then we went hurtling through these woods, clattered across an autobahn and fetched up in another bit of woodland on the far side, all breathless, hoarse, frightened, angry, confused and boiled to death.

If those Russians chased us, I wouldn't know because I was busy hanging on. And if there was any traffic on that autobahn, I also couldn't tell you because my eyes were shut. All I can tell you is that I was mighty glad when we stopped and reckoned we must have covered about three kilometres in about twenty seconds. And if anybody is interested, I have a recommendation for trainers: if you want to get the best out of your racehorse, take him on to a gunnery range just as they open fire, just before the Derby.

Thinking about it later I realised that what really upset the Kommandant was not only that we were swanning around on his gunnery range in the first place and horribly out of bounds, but I also remember crossing a bare piece of ground in those woods with little flags all over it – though we did it at full tilt – and thinking about it, I think it must have been a minefield.

Eastern Germany was full of fortifications of some kind and for the rest of that day, I heard those guns booming away and more in front as well. We also passed a grim place deep in those woods with a nasty-looking contraption of some sort in the middle all wired off, then past a house which had been all shot to pieces, with the roof blown off, windows shattered and furniture scattered all over the place outside, newish stuff.

Those woods were huge and we went through them all the way to Berlin on tracks. They were full of wild boar, I saw deer and the variety of trees was astounding. Then we'd break suddenly into huge empty spaces with these miradors everywhere, towers, which I took for look-out towers first of all, and imagined I'd managed to find my way on to some new gunnery range or bit of verboten territory, realising later they were for shooting: for the fat-cats of the communist world to take their leisurely time out and blaze away at the boar and deer while the masses slaved away.

It took three days to get to Berlin from Höchenwalde and those three nights were rough. I spent one on a pile of wet pig food, along with a lot of rats and I went hungry. The horses fared better.

The next night I spent out in the forest with them, and that was gloomy and wet. My second-to-last night was spent with a couple of seriously boozed up characters who farmed on the outskirts of Berlin and were looking forward to unification with mixed feelings. First it meant they'd lose their jobs on the collective and secondly it meant they'd have to find markets for the vegetables they grew. The idea of actually having to look for markets appalled them. No they said, they had enough trouble farming the blooming stuff; somebody else can sell it. But what did attract them about unification was that it meant they might get an offer on their land: they'd be rich!

West Germans were moving in, buying things, selling things, selling food – they whined – because the easterners were rejecting eastern foodstuffs, they complained, and so here were all these Brussels sprouts ten times the price being sold in the markets and they couldn't sell theirs! So they changed their tune and decided that unification was a rotten idea. It all made me think of Alexander back in Hungary and how he viewed Eastern Germany. A virgin market he called it. I rather fear that by the time Alexander gets there, and by the time he's got round to undoing his trousers, he'll find the virgin has already been had.

'*So mitte, so titte, sam sak, sak sak!*' my friends toasted, roaring with laughter. '*Prost!*' And we gargled away the last of the vodka.

And outside, the other side of the window, convoys of Russians were going home. Lorry after lorry droned past on wet cobbled streets.

My major source of worry tore at me as Karo, Puşa and I headed off towards Potsdam the following day, skirting an aerodrome. I was told I'd find signposts to West Berlin, or could ask and would know it anyway because of double-decker buses. Then I'd find the cavalry and throw myself on their mercy.

It didn't work out that way.

I saw this horsebox, a trailer on the side of the road, found out who owned it, explained I was broke, spent my last night in East Germany and the next day Heiko Sassenberg drove the three of us the three hundred and thirty kilometres to Göttingen and the miracle was, I discovered the wallet I thought I'd left in Czechoslovakia. It was in my numnah pocket which I'm sure I'd searched a thousand times before I was convinced my wallet had gone. In that wallet were 300 Deutschmarks, the cost of Heiko's transport, though I promised to send him 200 more as and when I could.

He took me to Juliette Mallison – she being the English vet I'd met way back in Hungary and who'd been brave enough to suggest I drop in on her on my way home. I bet she regrets it.

She stabled the horses, and me.

Vagabond

The shock of being back in the West was a big one.

Despite there having been western goods in East Germany it still had that worn-out feel about it I'd become so accustomed to. Nothing was painted, everything looked exhausted and old: pipework was shoddy, taps dripped and leaked, Trabant cars wheezed blue-smokily about the roads. There were no fences, the fields were all enormous – except in Poland – and generally, a kind of Third World feel was part of the psyche of the place, a feeling I had grown to know and expect.

Then, suddenly to see Persian rugs, oil paintings, paintings of ancestors, beautiful cabinets and oak bureaux was astonishing, as astonishing as the penury of the East. In Göttingen I found it hard to believe I was looking in a second-hand clothes shop at trousers which cost seventy pounds. I couldn't believe it. Mine were in tatters. I wear trousers until they fall apart, then give them secondary life as dusters. That someone should buy a pair of trousers for a few wearings then flog them struck me as astonishing.

It had been extraordinary arriving at the remains of the West German border, the difference beginning smack on that fence, now just a broken fence, a fence designed tragically to keep its people in, rather than anyone out, which to my mind shows the rottenness of the system from its onset.

No more were there people standing in fields hoeing, no more horses and carts, grubby little houses, peasant faces. The tree-lined rolling countryside round Göttingen with its red sandstone and beech forests, the order and cleanliness gave a feeling of wellbeing, of prosperity, certainty of direction. To arrive, for me, was a final indictment of communism and how it ruined all the countries it set out to control. That at best it could have been noble-minded, just badly thought out and incompetently run, but at worst and realistically it was little more than a malignant fraud exercised by despots, as bad or even worse than the tyrants they overthrew. I found it sad. Sad that people should have been so misled and for such a long time, as I found it equally moving when I saw three Russian soldiers in Frankfurt Oder walking round a store. It was a store which had recently been filled with goods from West Germany: expensive goods, nice things, good clothing, high quality stuff. These soldiers were walking round clutching roubles.

In due course they would have to return to their homes in Russia, where there is nothing, where the shops are as grim and empty as those I saw in Bulgaria (which, since I was there, has slung out the communist government, who, like others before them, lied about what they would do and brought nothing but shortage). I felt sorry for those soldiers, despite all that I had seen and been told, despite all the hatred and anger I'd heard directed at them. There was about the whole thing a fantastic tragedy being acted out in front of my eyes. There are other stories: of soldiers selling guns to buy food to take back to Russia, of deserters, of soldiers marrying German girls so as not to have to return; all sorts of things.

And there in the West, in all the plenty, suddenly confronted with all that is familiar, I heaved a huge sigh of relief. And I breathed it because albeit we consume too much, at least we have it and can make decisions and choices and direct our lives coherently and choose less if we want to because we are free to do so. And although I found much of what people had carved out for themselves in the East admirable, it was the absence of choice that was so devastating, and that the people were often unaware of it was incomprehensible to me.

I wandered round in a kind of a daze, while up in the riding stable a gorgeous girl called Stephanie Jarosch took charge of Karo and Puşa and I rode them for the last few times around the forestry and through the trees, beneath the autumn leaves and went one day for a long ride with Juliette and was as impressed with the German countryside as I was with the town. And it was with Juliette and Folker, their sons Robert and Peter and their wonderful grandma I celebrated Unification Day, and heard that they regarded it as the real end of the Second World War and that now they could set right the mistakes of the past forty years and invigorate a land which was essentially German with exactly the same rights and sovereignty as any state should be entitled to. They impressed me as a family, and I was impressed with Germany, with the industry of its people, with their generosity and wish to put the communist era behind them and get on with rebuilding.

I met a man down on the Danube when I was alone with Karo, and he told me he thought it would take ten years for Eastern Germany to fall in to line, to become truly integrated and to resolve their problems. I don't believe it: I think they'll do it in less than that, and what's more, I think Germany will extend that help into Russia and if Germany is bound to rise as a great world power, and I believe it will, it will rise as the greatest peace-making power the world has ever known.

When I talked to Juliette about it all I added that what struck me as incredible about Eastern Europeans was that to a man they are the most unobservant people I have ever encountered and told her of when Csabika and I went through the tunnel in Fuses bony, there was a man reading a newspaper who didn't see us until I asked him to move and those horses were making an incredible noise. How often do you see horses in railway pedestrian subways anyway? That wasn't an isolated experience. There were dozens like it.

'Simple!' she said. 'They've been conditioned not to think: therefore they don't see, certainly not inquisitively as we do.'

And Folker explained how the Treuhandstalt, which is a kind of government trust department, will handle the sale of nationalised industries in East Germany, how the Bundesbank has increased its loan increment and is offering attractive loans to people to get going in business in the East. Heiko Sassenberg was a case in point: his horsebox he'd bought on a 100 per cent loan. Already the German government had promised that when the Russians take all their soldiers back Germany will supply the cash for them to buy homes.

Folker was interesting about East German business people who were utterly confused by western business methods, and nervous because now their jobs were threatened. Merit was the key word now, not just function. Like many that I had met, the idea of having to look for and find markets was anathema to them, of having to produce goods to sell at competitive prices, a system completely at odds with all they knew – even top management. But, he said, there were good opportunities and for the prudent, advantages to be had. Of land, collectives were being rented off piecemeal – as Rima was doing – or in some cases handed back to former owners, which was a thorny problem.

And so the unification party went on, and my trip was finished.

Next day I'd managed to get a transfer of cash and with it bought myself a ticket, said goodbye to Karo and Puşa and went back to England.

I arrived in sunshine, as I had left, and Chumpie met me at the airport. It was strange to see her, strange to be in England.

Seven days later she took me back to my cottage up on the Borders where Mark Alderson was staying with my bull terrier Punch, and it was good to see them both. Punch, as I'd guessed, had been a bit of a problem. I read a letter, which Punch, wrote to Bill, Mark's own bull terrier. It went:

'Dear Bill,

I'm afraid I just couldn't resist them. You see I found this lovely pair of silky knickers peeking out of a pile of laundry. Luckily, I was on my own in the house at the time, and was able to do all sorts of disgusting things to them before chewing them to shreds in a frenzy of delightful ecstasy.

Yours, etc.'

There are other letters and he did worse things. I haven't, as yet, had any bills from Mark but maybe he's waiting for me to scrape a few bob together.

That afternoon I went to look for Dolly, who I knew would be around in the fields somewhere and I found her just over the hill. She answered when I called though was confused. I hadn't seen her for six months but she was every bit as pretty as I remember with her big dark eyes and that lovely Welsh dished face. She came home and went straight to the barn and immediately called out for Gonzo, who the next day I went to get. And because I have no horsebox, Chumpie took me. Gonzo didn't recognise me for a moment either, but he tumbled when I bit his nose. Everyone has a little trick, don't they?

And I can tell that look of recognition in a horse's eye: especially his: we've travelled a long way together, Gonzo and I.

Jane and Arabella Lennox had looked after him well: it's easy to spot. They'd not tried to slap him about or change his personality but accepted him for his funny Criollo ways, his sharpness and, sometimes, unpredictability. That they should have left him as they found him, as himself, is for me the mark of horsemanship. Horsewomanship.

Jane rode with me for an hour or two along the lanes toward my home then turned back and Gonzo went straight on because he knew he was going home. He'd walked that road once before, six months before, but he knew the way back and all I did was sit on him.

He and Dolly met like lovers from seasons apart, the flying front feet, snorts of indignation for months of absence – you can hear all these tones, they're all there.

And so life returned to normal once again and once again I went down to The Crown to have a drink with Jeff and John Morris and Jock, and had dinner with the Beesleys, and went to see John Napper and Pauline and drank too much there too and nobody asked any questions, and it was as if I'd never left the valley, which is how I like it.

And my ten pounds went a long way.

I was completely broke.

And somehow, the whole thing wasn't resolved: there wasn't a conclusion: I didn't quite know what to think of the things I'd seen, being caught up instead in Conservative party leadership contests, the crisis in the Gulf and the very terrible threat I felt Saddam Hussein presented, the ace card he might have held up his sleeve, but had not yet played.

Looking back on the trip, it was worthwhile but what had been worthwhile for me was not just the people I'd met but, for all the wrongness of communism in its operative form, the people were kind. There was heart in the villages which seems to have gone from ours, they had community and a sense of belonging which you seldom feel in

English society today in the degree in which it was obvious in Eastern Europe. But maybe that's a symptom of having to depend on your neighbour because of the lack of communication away from the village. Or maybe it's because our television sets have replaced our neighbours and we don't need to know them since we get all the information we think we need over the air. I don't know: I just know the feeling in the villages over there was a good one.

And the real Velvet Revolution must be East Germany, because unlike the others, they're getting the pieces picked up for them: they hold Europe's strongest and most influential currency, they have the backing of Europe's richest country and all the vigour of those people who, however you think of them, you have to concede they are enormously talented and know where they're going.

I didn't meet any obvious nationalist feeling in Germany while I was there except on one occasion when in the company of a man who was clearly nationalistic and loathed foreigners, and that was a nasty feeling. It's sad that the most forceful people in life are also the most stupid and that man made a lot of noise for one so abominably short of brains.

Enough of that.

I rode Gonzo round the lanes with Punch tagging along behind and watched winter coming to the hills. I watched the very tail end of summer colours fade away in the oaks in the fields round about and the buzzards gliding above them, and thought of Karo and Puşa.

I thought of them the whole time.

When I sold Rooster all those years ago, I knew it for a mistake immediately and then, on a sad day in Turkey when I sold Şimşek and Ahmed Paşa I tried to think of ways in which I could keep them, take them with me and I still think about them, still wonder where they are, how they are. And I think of Maria in Greece, the little black filly, although I know where she is and who owns her and what good hands she's in, but for all the world, I would sooner she were in mine.

Karo and Puşa had become a great part of me and the day I left them in Germany was a great wrench because I know that look in a horse's eye, and find it hard to take. I remember the look Little Pink gave me when I sold him. He knew I was selling him. I don't know how he knew, but he knew. Little Pink. If I had the money, I'd go and get Little Pink – all of them.

And now the months have passed and the fields are bare and frosted in the morning, grey and sharp and cold.

It's 3.30 in the morning and I have blood on my hands.

But for me this is a joy.

For this is the blood of birth.

At 12.30 last night I hung an oil lamp up over the manger in the barn. I have no electricity here and use oil lamps. And I kept going back and forth to the barn, in and out, checking. I don't know how many times I've been over to the barn tonight.

Then just an hour ago, by the light of that lamp, I foaled a mare, a mare with a hogged mane. And the foal is exactly like her mother, with a broad forehead and neat little muzzle, with little short cannons to the front and big long shannons to the rear.

And I watched as she struggled to her feet and wobbled around in the darkness on her long legs and I wiped her clean and her mother let me because she and I are old friends: we've been a long way together. And in one corner of the barn watching through the gloom, standing quietly in the darkness was a black horse, a black gypsy horse with number 316 tattooed on his side and in the other corner was a Criollo gelding and a little Welsh pony, and they were silent all the way through as that mare heaved and pushed and had her foal. They knew what was going on. Then the black horse came over and sniffed the foal and the mare let him, because they're old friends, and they have been a long way together. In fact, they're inseparable.

I telephoned André even though it was the middle of the night and he's coming here to see the foal and I don't know how he's done it, but he's got a bottle of țuica.

7 a.m.

André left half an hour ago.

We went into the barn together as soon as he came and took the țuica and André poured a little into his hands and rubbed it over the little foal's head and gave her a name. And we drank a toast to the foal and to her mother and to the black horse. We drank a toast to the man who'd sold us the mare and to the gypsy who'd sold the black horse.

And we drank a toast to the countries they came from, to the sun that shone on them, to the people of those countries, to the mountains we crossed and to the wells we drank from and to the good man who made the țuica. Then we drank a toast to the foal again, and said her name, because she is well-named, and the name we gave her was what we were, how we travelled, what the foal's mother was, what the black horse was, how we lived and what we became because we didn't have the cash to be anything else, and I wouldn't have changed that for the world.

Acknowledgements

PUŞA: This it then?

SIR KARO: S'pose so.

PUŞA: This where Fishface lives?

SIR KARO: S'pose so.

PUŞA: Told you he was a gypsy.

SIR KARO: But look! Look!

PUŞA: What? What?

KARO: It's Trapalanda! Horses' Heaven!

FISHFACE: Karo and Puşa – thank you. Thank you from the bottom of my heart.

My thanks also to:

KEITH BRYAN SADDLES, WALSALL, BIRMINGHAM, TEL: 01922 628325. Thank you Keith for supplying my *PATHFINDER saddles*. No bullshit: they're the best. They sat on the horses' backs for 4,500 kilometres and still look new, and I gave them a hell of a hammering.

The Pathfinder saddle has a quilted goatskin seat with high cantle, a long tree to spread weight, the underside being cowhide, the flaps pigskin. Somehow, they fit any horse.

211

I hear you won the Master Saddler's competition again, Keith. Tell me something new.

ANDRÉ BUBEAR, andrebub@yahoo.co.uk
Thanks André for those superbly crafted saddlebags, the *Bubear* on the backs of the saddles, which is a raised mild steel platform rising from the saddle fins which picks the saddlebags up off the horse's quarters: you get no rubbing at all, and the saddlebags hang evenly on the seat dispersing the weight along its length. I had not one problem with the whole caboodle and thoroughly recommend your work.

JANET CROSS, TIVERTOn, Devon. Thank you Janet for the waterproof gear and chaps which replaced my dreadful army ponchos: your kit is good. Without wishing to sound crackers, I convey a note of personal thanks from Karo and Puşa who would have gone mad without your fly screens that covered their eyes and ears, which did the trick and kept the flies off. I still have them.

HAWKINS ENDURANCE BOOTS, NORTHAMPTON
Roy Martinyak, who supplied my *riding boots*. They have a clever sole which means you can ride and walk in them. They have canvas sides so were cool in the sun. They lasted the whole distance and a lot more besides, since I'm still wearing them.

GREATER MANCHESTER MOUNTED POLICE
It might seem a funny place to say thanks to you all, particularly Bob and Nita, my instructors. Long distance riding and police work have a couple of things in common and they're both the horses – thanks for everything you did for me, for the training, an enjoyable fortnight and I don't care what the bosses say, I maintain a bobby on a horse is a horseman first and then a bobby.

Thanks Norman Brown for fixing it up, Ray Jackson for the red wine, Inspector Tony Buckley for instruction in skill-at-arms and Chief Inspector Paul Teasdale for arranging it all.

NEIL MCCARRAHERS, BROOKWOOD, SURREY
Thanks for those cotton towelling numnahs and your help all down the line.

SUUNTO COMPASS: Nobody gave me one, I bought one myself. They're damn good compasses.

CECILIA HUMPHRYS
Thanks, Chumpie, for bailing me out all along the line, all those frantic telephone calls to save me from going completely broke, for fixing up André and Gavin and everything else. Big kiss from Karo – he's your horse.

COLONEL ZOG ZVEGINTSOV and CARRIE, You helped me more than you knew, much more. Let's go and get that tank, Zog.

FOLKER and JULIETTE MALLISON, I bet you really regret that little invitation to drop in on you. Thank you Juliette and Folker for coping with me and the horses: nice vetting Juliette, thank you.

STEPHANIE JAROSCH Big kisses from us all – you did a wonderful job of looking after both Karo and Puşa in Göttingen: come and stay.

RACEHORSE TRANSPORTERS ASSOCIATION
Thanks Rick Bridgland for the effort you put into the shipment of the horses back home.

STEVE CASS and ANDRÉ BUBEAR
Thanks Steve for all that driving and André for fixing up the barter, Steve for swinging the barter and Sue for the truck.

KEN LUNN, CLUNSIDE GARAGE, CLUN
Thanks Ken for the welding job on the back of the saddles: that was a tricky piece of work. Your welding put up with a lot of thumping and held the whole way.

MARK EVANS D.W.C.F.

Thanks for sorting out all those feet Mark and you can give me a set of shoes for free advertising.

There are plenty of other names but they're in the script and if they're not, they're in my heart and you'll find them there.

Thanks as ever to St Christopher, St Anthony, St Hypolitus and St Jude.